Lester B. Pearson

Susan Hughes

Fitzhenry & Whiteside

Contents

Chapter		Page
1	From Lester to Mike	3
2	Finding a Path	9
3	The Civil Servant: 1928-1939	15
4	Quiet Diplomacy: 1939-1948	21
5	The Golden Age of Diplomacy: 1948-1957	29
6	A Losing Leader: 1957-1958	36
7	Dief the Chief: 1958-1963	41
8	Prime Minister Pearson	47
9	The Second Term	54
10	Pearson's Legacy	60
	Timeline	62
	Further Reading	64
	Credits	64
	Index	64

THE CANADIANS®
A Continuing Series

Lester B. Pearson

Author: Susan Hughes
Cover Illustration: John Mardon
Design: KerryDesigns

THE CANADIANS® *is a registered trademark of Fitzhenry & Whiteside Limited.*

Fitzhenry & Whiteside acknowledges with thanks the Canada Council for the Arts, the Government of Canada through its Book Publishing Industry Development Program, and the Ontario Arts Council for their support of our publishing program.

National Library of Canada Cataloguing in Publication
Hughes, Susan, 1960-
Lester B. Pearson / Susan Hughes.
(The Canadians)
Includes index.
ISBN 1-55041-504-2

1. Pearson, Lester B., 1897-1972--Juvenile literature.
2. Canada--Politics and government--1963-1968--Juvenile literature. 3. Canada--Politics and government--1957-1963--Juvenile literature. 4. Canada--Politics and government--1935-1957--Juvenile literature. 5. Prime ministers--Canada--Biography--Juvenile literature.
I. Title. II. Series: Canadians.

FC621.P4H83 2003   j971.064'3'092   C2003-903422-4

© 2004 Fitzhenry & Whiteside Limited
195 Allstate Parkway, Markham, Ontario L3R 4T8

Chapter 1
From Lester to Mike

"What do you want to be when you grow up?" If anyone had asked the young Lester Pearson, he would never have answered, "Prime Minister of Canada." He would never have answered, "a politician" or "a civil servant." It was far more likely he would have said, "A Methodist minister, like my father," or "A sports hero."

Lester Bowles Pearson was born on April 23, 1897 in Newtonbrook, Ontario. This small community was next to Toronto, which would boom in population from about 100,000 in 1880 to over 200,000 in 1901. About twenty years earlier, Alexander Graham Bell had invented the telephone and two years before Lester's birth, Guglielmo Marconi had successfully sent the first wireless message in Morse code across the Atlantic Ocean. Now telephone and electricity wires were beginning to stretch across the streets of Toronto, and Toronto's street railways were slowly converting from being horse-drawn to being powered by wires strung along trolley poles.

In Newtonbrook, however, Lester saw only horses and buggies travelling the roads with just the occasional motorcar rattling past. And it wasn't until Lester was five that the Wright brothers, Orville and Wilbur, flew the first heavier-than-air vehicle in a sustained flight.

At the turn of the century, Canada was still an active part of the British Empire, which contained nearly one-quarter of the earth's population and covered one-quarter of the earth's land surface. Queen Victoria had ruled Britain and its colonies since 1837, and few Canadians could remember another monarch. Monuments to her were everywhere, and her name graced parks, streets, hospitals, counties—Victoria, British

Wilfrid Laurier

Columbia, was even named after her. Lester's home may have had a coloured print of Queen Victoria hanging on the wall. Certainly his school classroom did.

The Empire permitted nationhood to take root in its overseas colony in 1867. Confederation transformed all of the various bits and pieces of British North America into one country—Canada. There were two levels of government put into place: each province had its own government to take care of local matters, and there was a federal government in Ottawa for the whole country. The House of Commons was made up of members of Parliament elected from each part of the country. (Women, however, were not allowed to vote then or even by the time of Pearson's birth.) The party with the most members of Parliament chose a prime minister. There was also a Senate, which was comprised of people appointed by the prime minister, not elected by the people.

Canada was physically diverse and vast—three thousand miles [4,800 km] from sea to sea. Political parties had to attract support right across the country, attempting to appeal to each region and province. When Pearson was born, Wilfrid Laurier, leader of the Liberal party, had been prime minister for one year. Confederation guaranteed equal status to French and English, but still there was tension between the mainly French-speaking Catholic population of Quebec and the rest of the country, which was primarily English-speaking and Protestant. Despite this friction, the French-Canadian and Catholic Laurier would retain the confidence of enough of a cross-section of the Canadian people to remain prime minister for fifteen years.

Lester's parents were supporters of the Conservative party. Like many Canadians, they believed that Canada was best served by remaining firmly attached to the British crown. In this way, their sense of nationalism was strongly tied to their imperialism. Lester himself grew up sharing these political views, but he couldn't recall much political discussion during the early years in his household. "I was more concerned with getting good marks, playing shinny, or catching fly balls, and even more with becoming the greatest all-round athlete Canada had ever produced," he wrote in his memoirs.

(L-R): Annie Pearson, Lester Pearson, age 2, Marmaduke Pearson on tricycle, Ed Pearson holding Vaughan

Lester Pearson's family consisted of his mother, Annie, his elder brother, Marmaduke (or Duke), his younger brother, Vaughan, and his father, Edwin. Methodists were the largest Protestant sect, and the wealthiest, in Canada in 1900, and Ed was an itinerant Methodist minister. Because Ed was permitted only a three-year term in any one area, the Pearson family moved often. They remained within southern Ontario, however, and the communities in which they lived were similar in their British origins and Anglo-Canadian culture.

Lester Pearson remembered: "To a boy, there were advantages and disadvantages in moving so much. There was hardly time to take root or become attached to a house and community. But against this there were new scenes, new people, new experiences. I was fortunate in being able to adjust easily, and make new friends. The Ontario school system was always very much the same wherever we lived. So were the church and the parsonage, at least to the children of the family. Home was always warm and secure."

Lester's father had much more money than most Canadians, yet Lester noted: "We did not need movies, radio, or television to help us pass the time, for we never had enough time for all the things we wished to do ... Our greatest pleasures cost us nothing." Fun was balanced with work. As they grew older, Lester and his brothers helped out at home with chores and Lester took over a local paper route.

Lester enjoyed school and was exceptionally intelligent, often standing near the top of the class. His remarkable memory helped him excel in subjects such as Latin, English grammar, and history. Lester was also a fine athlete who liked to play and liked to win. A good game of lacrosse or rugby also helped him unleash his frustration and aggression. But baseball, which had become Canada's most popular summer sport, was also Lester's favourite and that of his brothers and father, and this common interest was a bond between them.

In 1913 Lester graduated from Hamilton Collegiate Institute at sixteen years of age. Now the question "What do you want to be when you grow up?" most certainly was being asked of him. Or then again, maybe not. Maybe his parents didn't even bother to ask Lester what he thought. "My parents, for some reason or other, hoped that I, of the three sons, would continue the ministerial tradition in the family," he recalled in his memoirs. But he went on to note: "They were to be disappointed. In this respect I let them down."

Lester did, however, follow his older brother to Victoria College in the University of Toronto, a Methodist foundation and his father's alma mater. He did well his first year academically and on the sports field. But before the autumn of his second year, events in Europe had spun out of control. At the end of June, 1914, the archduke of Austria-Hungary and heir to the throne, Franz Ferdinand, and his wife were assassinated in the Bosnian town of Sarajevo. Austria-Hungary blamed Serbia and declared war on that country. Russia allied with the Serbs, and the French supported the Russians. Germany backed Austria and attacked France and then Belgium, a neutral country.

Britain was an ally of France and had promised to defend Belgium's neutrality. On August 4, 1914, the king of England, King George V, declared war against Germany on behalf of all the British Empire. And Canada? In 1899, fifteen years previous, it was assumed by Britain that Canada would send troops to South Africa, a British colony, in support of a British war effort. But Prime Minister Wilfrid Laurier had stalled, choosing to let the Canadian Parliament decide whether or not to get involved. The two-day debate in the cabinet was a divisive one. Many French Canadians didn't wish to participate in an imperialist war. Many English Canadians, loyal to the Crown, strongly believed that they should fight shoulder to shoulder with the British. They believed the delay in sending troops was unspeakable. On October 13, 1899, Laurier reached what he felt was a compromise. Canada would equip and send a volunteer force of 1,000 men to serve with the British. Many Canadians were disappointed— those who felt strongly that Canada had sold out and shouldn't be sending any troops overseas, and those who felt strongly that Laurier was not doing enough to support Britain. A French-Canadian anti-imperialist nationalism began to blossom in Quebec. Nevertheless, in 1911, the Conservative party led by Robert Borden won the federal election, having campaigned on a pro-British platform and claiming Laurier was not patriotic enough.

Now, three years later, Britain was declaring war and again looking to Canada to fall in step. Constitutionally, Canada had no foreign policy of its own, and Borden's election persuaded him that most English Canadians considered themselves British. When Britain declared war, Canada rushed to its defence without hesitating.

Thousands of civilians hurried to enlist. Both Lester and Duke joined the University Officers Training Corps when they returned to school in September. Studying was impossible. The young men, longing to be overseas, were distracted by their sense of unfulfilled duty to their country. Near the end of February, Duke enlisted with the 25th Battery, Canadian Field Artillery and on April 23, 1915, Lester signed up with the University of Toronto Hospital Unit. His parents gave their underage son their permission only because the unit was non-combative.

Lester B. Pearson serving with the Canadian Army Medical Corps

Lester was sent to England in May. Shortly after, his unit headed east, landing in Salonika in Macedonia on November 12, 1915. Greece was neutral, however British and French troops were stationed there, mainly to prevent the Bulgarians from reaching their German allies. Lester's contribution was minor and he wanted to be doing more. He wanted to fight in France. The young man wrote to his father, asking him to speak to Ed's friend, Sam Hughes, Canada's minister of militia, about getting an infantry commission and on February 19, 1917, Lester received orders to return to England.

By March 30, 1917, Lester was an officer cadet in D Company, No. 4 Officer Cadet Battalion in Oxford. When he completed training at the end of July, he was a lieutenant. But Lester simply ended up at Bramshot Camp with his brother, Duke, commanding a platoon, still waiting impatiently to go overseas and see some real action.

Finally, Lester applied for a transfer and, that fall, reported for training in the Royal Flying Corps (RFC). The RFC was a dangerous area of service where life expectancy was measured in months. Two important changes would occur while he was with the RFC.

"If Lester is my name, Mike is what I am usually called. This change goes back to World War I when I was training with the RFC. My Squadron Commander felt that Lester was no name for an aspiring fighter pilot and decided to call me Mike. It stuck, and I was glad to lose Lester."

Lester's name changed—and his life changed too. Just before Christmas, while on leave in London, Pearson was hit by a bus. After some convalescent time, he was put on leave. On April 6, 1918, just before his twentieth birthday, the young man was sent home to Canada.

As well as being injured physically, Pearson had suffered a nervous breakdown. Perhaps it was induced by the anxious months of waiting to go to France and the subsequent stressful months of training to fly. "It was a time I shall never forget. It was then that I became an adult. I began to think of things beyond the pleasures and excitements, the troubles and fears of the moment. I began to think, for the first time, about the war in its deeper significance and to realize its full horrors and gruesome stupidities ... We [Lester and his friend, Clifford Hames] spent hours trying to get some understanding of what we were being asked to do; to bring some reason to the senseless slaughter. For what? King and country? Freedom and democracy? These words sounded hollow now in 1918 and we increasingly rebelled against their hypocrisy. The fighting would go on and on. We, who were trapped in it, would also go on and on until we joined the others already its victims."

Plagued by nightmares, Pearson had spent his last months in England re-evaluating his war experiences and his role as a participant. He would never be the same, would never be able to become close emotionally to others or to sustain intense commitments to any faith or ideology.

Chapter 2
Finding a Path

The war had now lasted three years. Clearly Canada was making an important contribution to the war effort, providing both munitions and hundreds of thousands of troops. But although the Canadian government was responsible for recruiting, training, transporting, equipping, and paying for the soldiers, it had little control over their deployment and use. Then, in February 1917, Canadian prime minister Robert Borden and other premiers of the dominions were asked by the recently elected British prime minister David Lloyd George to sit as members of the new Imperial War Cabinet. During the Imperial War Conference in March, the dominion prime ministers, for the first time, were actually given an inside look at Britain's war effort and, also for the first time, their opinions were heard (although largely ignored). Canada, and the other dominions, were asked, and most agreed, to contribute more troops against the threat of a stronger Germany. The Conference ended with an adopted resolution, proposed by Borden, to hold a special imperial conference after the war to discuss new status for the dominions within the commonwealth. Instead of being self-governing colonies, they would become partners within the empire-commonwealth, "autonomous nations of an Imperial Commonwealth." (This was the first time the term "commonwealth" was used officially.)

When the war ended on November 11, 1918, 60,000 Canadians were dead, 173,000 wounded, and a total of 650,000 men and women had served in the forces. Pearson had been home for about seven months. The air force had kept him on in the service as an aerial navigation instructor. With the war over, he was put on paid leave from December 1918 to April 1919, which meant he had sufficient funds to return to university. All veterans returning from the war were automatically given one year's credit, which meant that Pearson needed only one more year to complete his degree. He was starting mid-year but the University of Toronto agreed that he could pick up the whole year's credit between January and May.

Meanwhile, the peace talks were set to begin in Paris between the four major allies and victors of the war—Britain, France, the United States, and Italy. For a time, it seemed that the gains made by the dominions were at risk. Lloyd George was reluctant to let them help shape the peace, proposing that one voice, Canada's Borden, represent all the dominions and be the fifth delegate at the Paris Peace Conference. Borden refused, insisting on full representation for each dominion as part of the British delegation. The Americans, wondering why Canada should be represented at all, were reminded that Canadians had actually lost more troops in the war than the Americans.

Finally the American President, Woodrow Wilson, proposed that two delegates each from Canada, South Africa, Australia, and India take part. However, because of their "inferior" status as part nation, part colony, and part imperial colleagues, the voices of the dominions were muted, just as they had been at the Imperial War Conference in 1917, and the dominions contributed little to the final peace treaty.

It was at this post-war Paris Peace Conference that the League of Nations was established. Lester Pearson would one day become very involved with this new international body. The League was founded on the principle of collective or group security for the purpose of averting war. Aggression against any one member would be considered aggression against all members ("all for one and one for all") and might result in economic or military measures taken by all against the aggressor. Why? The hope was that this would act as a deterrent against aggression. The hope was that any nation considering attacking a weak nation would think no further, knowing that other League nations would immediately come to the aid of the weaker nation. The League was further dedicated to the preservation of peace through the arbitration of international disputes. At its formation, Prime Minister Borden insisted that Canada be a member in the League of Nations' General Assembly, as well as being eligible for membership in its governing council.

So peace had returned to Canada and in June 1919, twenty-two-year-old Lester Pearson, a war veteran and more experienced in the ways of the world, graduated from the University of Toronto with a Bachelors of Arts degree.

"What do you want to be when you grow up?" The question had more and more urgency for Pearson.

A minister? At some point, his parents had dropped their ambitions for him to follow in his father's footsteps. It must have been a relief for Pearson, especially since his faith had vanished during his time in Europe, surrounded by the horrors of war.

Now the sky was the limit. But the young man had no strong passion steering him and was uncertain about his future. He pondered several possibilities and wondered if law might appeal to him. Pearson arranged to article with a local law firm and gave it a try, but after only one week there, he bowed out. He knew right away that it wasn't for him.

Still at loose ends several weeks later and anxious to do something productive, Pearson turned to his uncle, Edson White, an executive with a large Chicago business, Armour and Company. During the war, Uncle Edson had promised to help Lester, if ever he needed it, in finding a job and now he came through for his nephew. In the fall of 1919, Pearson headed to Chicago where he was put on the stuffing line in the sausage department. It didn't sound like much, but it was a job that might lead to a career in business.

With many veterans on the hunt for work, Pearson was fortunate to get a job, and he stuck it out for several seasons. But during this time, he thought more about his aspirations, and in the winter of 1920, Pearson decided he wanted to go back to school. He wished to attend Oxford University in England and then teach history or political science at a university. Pearson applied for the Massey Foundation Fellowship, was interviewed by his former university don of pre-war days and commanding officer, Vincent Massey, and was awarded the fellowship about two weeks later. He applied to, and was accepted at, St. John's College at Oxford. In the fall of 1921, Pearson set sail for England.

"Seldom are expectations so completely fulfilled as were those of my two years at Oxford. I loved it all ..."

Pearson spent two years studying history, developing an

Oxford University vs. Switzerland hockey game. Pearson is at right front.

interest in "international relations," and playing college sports, especially hockey. When he returned to Toronto, Pearson was pleased to be offered a position as a lecturer in modern history at the University of Toronto. It was what he had hoped for, and he quickly accepted. On September 26, 1923, Lester Pearson gave his first lecture at the university.

One of the new teacher's students was Maryon Moody, a bright young woman from Winnipeg. Although it was not considered proper for a teacher to have a relationship with a student, Lester and Maryon fell in love soon after meeting and a month later were engaged. They kept their plans private however until Maryon graduated. Then she returned home to Winnipeg while Pearson continued to teach. On August 22, 1925, Lester and Maryon were married, and she was able to join him in Toronto.

As well as teaching, Pearson was expected to produce a thesis. In the summer of 1926, he headed to Ottawa to make use of the Public Archives in researching the United Empire Loyalists. As it happened, Canada's greatest constitutional drama was about to unfold in front of his eyes. William Lyon Mackenzie King, the Liberal leader, had been prime minister since 1921. The Liberals had won re-election the previous year, 1925, but they did not hold a majority in Parliament. Now, months later, a major scandal broke out and King's government seemed on the verge of a defeat in Parliament. As a result, the prime minister went to the Governor General, Lord Byng, and asked him to call a new election. Byng refused. Instead he chose to ask Arthur Meighen's Conservative party to form a government. King angrily resigned.

While parliament debated Byng's decision, Lester Pearson watched, fascinated, from the visitor's gallery for days. King was a firm monarchist but now he asked the public to consider who was really ruling Canada: an appointed British governor general or an elected government? The fight was between imperialism and nationalism, and the ongoing theme of Canada's relationship with Britain intrigued Pearson.

Double wedding of Grace Moody and Norman Young (left) and Maryon Moody and Lester Pearson (right)

His Ottawa experience influenced Pearson in another important way as well. Just before he left the capital, Pearson met a man who would be extremely influential in his professional life. Dr. O.D. Skelton was a former professor and foreign-policy consultant. King had appointed him the undersecretary of state for Canada's department of external affairs in 1925. He was now the prime minister's closest advisor and the leading civil servant of his time, not only influencing foreign policy but also domestic matters.

Until 1909, Britain retained responsibility for Canada's treaty negotiations with other countries or boundary disputes. Then, in 1909, Prime Minister Sir Wilfrid Laurier created Canada's own department of external affairs. However for many years external affairs had very limited functions and almost nothing at all to do with foreign policy. In 1912, the department was placed under the prime minister, giving it new prestige and greater authority, but its scope was still limited.

Canada was still strongly tied to Britain but was gradually growing in autonomy. Now, King, as both prime minister and minister of external affairs, and Skelton, his deputy minister, both wanted to transform the department into a genuine foreign office. King wanted Canada to be able to send its own diplomatic representatives abroad. He saw to it that Canadian legations (which became embassies) were opened in Washington, Paris, and Tokyo, and a Dominion of Canada

Advisory Office was opened in Geneva.

Skelton, who believed Canada must take control of its own affairs, was looking for bright, educated people for the civil service. He encouraged Pearson to think about leaving his teaching career and working for the government. In 1928, when a position at the external affairs department opened, Pearson applied. He wrote the four days of civil service exams in June and received the highest marks of any competitor. He was promptly offered, and accepted, the position of First Secretary.

Within weeks, the university countered with the offer of a promotion to full professor and a pay raise, but Pearson had made up his mind. He and Maryon had one child, Geoffrey, and another on the way. The Ottawa salary was higher, and, as Pearson noted significantly, "I thought also of my increasing interest in international affairs, and the new responsibilities which Canada would be assuming in the great and new world of foreign relations." Lester Pearson entered the civil service to begin a thirty-year career as a diplomat, and Canada would never be the same.

Dr. O.D. Skelton and Lester Pearson

Chapter 3
The Civil Servant: 1928-1939

A t thirty-one years of age, Pearson was eager to serve his country in his new capacity as civil servant. He would be working within a government department, external affairs, serving the deputy minister, Skelton, and, along with the rest of the staff, helping to develop, implement, and enforce government policies. This often meant clipping newspapers, running errands, and writing countless memoranda for Skelton.

Very focused and extremely hard working, Pearson learned quickly on the job. After almost a year in the Ottawa office, he was eager to be sent into the field. He spent the summer of 1929 in Washington, his first diplomatic posting, and returned to Ottawa in the fall. In January 1930, Pearson had his first international assignment, arriving in Britain as a delegate to the London Naval Conference. Canada had only three ships and yet "there we were, five dominions [Canada and four others] sitting around the council table in perfect, if somewhat perplexing, sovereign equality with the Big Powers [Britain, Italy, France, United States, and Japan]." Canada's status was slowly beginning to change.

Pearson learned many lessons in the art of diplomacy at this conference. Some were to do with the limitations of experts and the governments they served. Sometimes the way something was done seemed to be as, or more, important than what was done. "I also began to observe, in a further essential stage of the diplomat's progress, that ... [t]o [the] older sovereignties, protocol seems often to be as important as power."

Pearson would learn many more diplomatic lessons throughout the 1930s. In August 1930, the Conservatives, led by R.B. Bennett, were elected to power. Because the civil service is non-partisan and civil servants are not allied with any

R.B. Bennett

particular political party, Pearson and the other department staff simply carried on, retaining their jobs and doing their best to serve the new government and their new minister of external affairs, Prime Minister Bennett.

Bennett gave Pearson new responsibilities. The Depression had begun with the crash of the New York stock market in October 1929 and was now affecting all aspects of Canadian life. Unemployment grew and incomes shrank. Pearson was appointed to serve as secretary on two royal commissions (in 1931 and 1934) that studied the effects of the Depression on Canada. Pearson's fifteen-hour workdays, seven days a week, impressed the other commission members, as did the quality of his labours. A former history student, Pearson had never before needed to examine domestic economic affairs. Nor had he been interested enough in cconomics to wish to do so. But now long months studying the background of Canada's economics and the impact of the Depression itself served to broaden Pearson's understanding of the economic aspects of his country.

Mostly though, during his seven years based in Ottawa, Pearson worked steadily as a foreign-service officer with the occasional trip abroad. In 1932, he was part of a Canadian delegation to a world disarmament conference in Geneva, home to the League of Nations. Canada's role in the League had not been stellar, to say the least. In the 1920s, King had been against efforts to strengthen its collective security arrangements and refused to sign anything that might commit Canada to help a nation under attack. King had, therefore, weakened the effectiveness of the League by keeping Canada uninvolved.

Worried by the threatening aspect of war, Pearson was eager to do what he could to influence the part Canada could play in the search for peace. But he was disappointed by the conference. It seemed there were irreconcilable differences of opinion between the member countries. "The basic difficulty, and this remains true of all disarmament discussions, arose out of the relationship between security and disarmament." It was like the chicken-and-egg argument. Which should come first? Would disarmament bring security, or did a sense of security need to come before disarmament was possible? Many delegates believed that it wasn't prudent to disarm until security was ensured by international action and agreement. Many others believed that only disarmament could lead to the sense of security that would enable the undertaking of new security commitments.

The discussions and disagreements continued for months. "It was not easy to keep one's idealism, sense of proportion, or even of humour, as the conference bogged down in sterile detail and in petty debating exchanges ... National fears, national rivalries, national ambitions proved far stronger than any sense of international solidarity, or even cooperation." Pearson despaired of progress being made toward peace and security by collective action through the League.

And then things got worse. In 1934, the League lost two members, Japan and Germany. (Germany was becoming increasingly militarized, and Adolf Hitler, leader of the Nazi party, had been elected the year before.) Italy was intending to wage war against Abyssinia (now Ethiopia), and Abyssinia, a member of the League, looked to the international body for protection.

When, in 1935, Italy did invade Abyssinia, Dr. W.A. Riddell, the Canadian advisory officer, led the way in attempting to condemn Italy as an aggressor and apply sanctions to force it to withdraw. Skelton disagreed but Pearson, Riddell, and G. Howard Ferguson, the head of the Canadian delegation, challenged him. Ferguson spoke directly to Prime Minister Bennett, and when Bennett gave Ferguson permission to act as he thought best, Ferguson voted to declare Italy an aggressor.

In the midst of all this, there was a federal election in Canada. Bennett's government fell and King's Liberal government was elected. When the League was discussing the nature of the sanctions against Italy, the Canadians, led by Pearson's colleague, Riddell, suggested that oil be one of the materials embargoed. The League began debating the "Canadian resolu-

Staff of the Canadian High Commission in the United Kingdom: (Front, L-R): Lester Pearson, Vincent Massey, Georges Vanier; (Rear, L-R): unknown, Charles Ritchie

tion," but King, learning of it and knowing that many Canadians, especially within Quebec, admired Italy's leader Benito Mussolini, insisted that Riddell had been acting without the new government's go-ahead.

As Pearson bitterly noted, "The Canadian government was by no means alone in its timid attitude toward sanctions, an attitude potentially fatal, of course, to their success." The League never did impose the oil embargo. Italy occupied Addis Ababa on May 7, 1936, and Abyssinia became another colony in Italy's African empire.

Likely King was reflecting the general Canadian mood, which was a decided lack of concern about collective security, Abyssinia, the League, or Hitler. Even Pearson, who believed in the principle of collective security and was enthusiastic when it seemed that the League might work, had reservations and became cautious when it seemed that League commitments could embroil Canada in wars that had little to do with its national interest. Nevertheless he commented with hindsight: "My own view is that the failure in 1935 of the members of the League of Nations, including Canada, to stand up to a single aggressor, had much to do with the world war in 1939."

During the fall of 1935, Pearson had been transferred to the Canadian High Commission in London as First Secretary (and third in command). The first few weeks, he worked under G. Howard Ferguson. Then Vincent Massey, long-standing friend of King and personal friend of the Royal Family, became the new High Commissioner.

Pearson remained posted in London until 1939. When the League of Nations collapsed in 1936, Pearson lost faith in the possibility of disarmament and collective security. During the four years he was in London, he became more and more con-

Prime Minister King (centre) visiting Berlin, June 1937

vinced that another war was inevitable and that Canada would be involved. He watched as Mussolini and Hitler signed an alliance. He watched as the Spanish Civil War erupted in 1936, and as Japan, confident that the West would do nothing to intervene (and correct in that assumption), invaded China in 1937.

He watched as Europe began to fall apart. Adolf Hitler, Germany's aggressive dictator, threatened to take over countries that he believed should belong to the Reich, the German empire—and then he proceeded to turn his threats into reality. Germany advanced on the German-speaking countries, including the Rhineland and Austria. Britain, with its ally, France, retreated, conceding inch by inch to Hitler's demands, wanting to "appease" Germany, convinced that anything was better than another war. The Canadian government strongly supported the course of appeasement, and Pearson's own views were mixed. Then Germany began to threaten Czechoslovakia.

Pearson noted: "As my views changed about the character of the Nazi menace and I became convinced of the likelihood, even the inevitability of war, I naturally became more concerned about the foreign policy of my country in its relation to this threat. That policy had been based on no prior commitments, no co-operation with London in defence arrangements which might lead to such commitments, or which might cause

Adolf Hitler

controversy and disunity in Canada ... While very few in Ottawa thought we could escape involvement in a major war if it came, any more than we could in 1914, there were some ... who believed that such involvement should and could be limited to minimum participation. This was a view that might have appealed to me as late as 1936 but, by 1939, it seemed both wrong and unrealistic."

Finally it became crystal clear to all that appeasement had failed. Now there could be no more caution.

At the Munich Conference in September 1938, Britain surrendered part of Czechoslovakia, eliciting a promise from Germany to go no further. The British prime minister, Neville Chamberlain, thought he had pulled the world back from the brink of war, buying "Peace in our time."

But in March 1939, Hitler marched into Prague, despite the promises he had made in Munich, and the Soviet Union struck an alliance with Germany in late August. Britain and France had pledged to use force if Czechoslovakia was attacked—but they didn't. And then on September 1, 1939, Germany invaded Poland. No longer able to turn a blind eye, Britain declared war on Germany on September 3.

And Canada's reaction? Canada, as an independent member country of a Commonwealth of Nations, refused to enter the war on Britain's coattails. Pearson, though personally believing that Canada must go to war at once, approved of the stand taken, as did most Canadians. Parliament was summoned, a vote was taken, and after a week of technical formalities, Canada's official declaration of war came on September 10, 1939.

Chapter 4
Quiet Diplomacy: 1939-1948

Prime Minister King insisted on a limited war effort on Canada's part. He achieved this for a time, but when, in the summer of 1940, the Allies were defeated in France and Belgium, it was impossible to remain reserved. The Canadian people were now fully alarmed—and, with the fall of France, Canada was suddenly Britain's chief ally. The Canadian government vigorously responded, stepping up recruitment for the army, converting the economy to war production, rushing every available aircraft and ship overseas, and providing huge amounts of money to Britain.

Pearson remained concerned with Canada's role as an involved nation. Perhaps it was too much to hope for Canada's voice to have an influence, but Pearson believed his country should be consulted or, at the least, informed of decisions being made about a war to which it was now heavily committed. Before this, "it was difficult to remove the impression that we were once more supplying men and formations for 'imperial' forces under British management, or to convince our British friends that we had a legitimate national interest in the general conduct of the war and in the direction of its higher strategy, and that, at the very least, we had the right of a partner to know what was happening or not happening, and why." Much of Pearson's work in London was attempting to "change the colonial mentality" that existed in British thinking.

In January 1941, Dr. O.D. Skelton died, and King appointed Norman Robertson, six years Pearson's junior, as Skelton's replacement as undersecretary in external affairs. Pearson was extremely disappointed that he had not been chosen, but he reluctantly, loyally, agreed when asked by Prime Minister King to return to Ottawa to be one of three assistant under-

King, Roosevelt and Churchill meet during World War II

secretaries. In his new position, Pearson was head of the Commonwealth and European division of the department of external affairs; he sat on many interdepartmental boards and he had to deal with internal security matters. Pearson was also becoming increasingly involved in tending the growing relationship between the United States and Canada. Although the United States had not yet plunged into the European war and was still officially neutral, the war and increasing concerns about their own security were forging a closer relationship between the U.S. and Canada. Just the previous summer, in August 1940, President Roosevelt and King had met and set up the Permanent Joint Board on Defence, which would report to the governments on how best to defend North America. But the relationship between the countries was a delicate one—Pearson and King wanted to cooperate with the United States without moving too close to their neighbour. They worried about the huge southern nation absorbing Canada.

When Japan attacked Pearl Harbor in Oahu, Hawaii, on December 7, 1941, the United States entered the war. The European war became a world war. Canada became involved with the United States as an ally, and, as Pearson noted: "We had to be careful here, however, as in London, to insist that we should be treated not as a subordinate to be ordered, but as an ally to be asked and consulted ... If occasionally Washington acted as though Canada were another state of the union, we tried to be tolerant, realized that our American friends, unlike the British, had not been educated to respect our national sovereign status—and our sensitivity. They too would learn this, under our firm but friendly teaching, or so we hoped."

Well, it was not so easy, as Pearson would find out first-hand. Despite its sizeable participation in the war, Canada ultimately was left out of the higher war strategy and decision-making after 1941. At first, Pearson worried about Canada being squeezed between the United States and Britain. "During the war, however, our difficulty was more often to avoid being squeezed out [altogether] ..." President Roosevelt and Prime Minister Winston Churchill had become fast friends and were jointly directing the war effort, with little interest in Canadian opinion.

In 1942, Pearson was sent to Washington, where he would remain throughout the war, as Minister-Counsellor in the Legation under Leighton McCarthy. Pearson was pleased, describing the city as "an exciting place to live and work" and "the centre of the whole Allied war effort." While taking every opportunity to educate Americans about Canada, he also dealt with the press, wrote speeches, and covered the State Department.

Pearson's major concerns were with wartime military, economic, and political problems. Britain, Pearson believed, had invaluable international experience and qualities of restraint and calmness, qualities Pearson felt the United States lacked. The possibility of the loss of Britain's influence in the international arena worried him for a time. By the winter of 1943, he was convinced that the United States and the Soviet Union would dominate the world when the war was finished. As the United States grew in world power and influence and Britain's strength declined, Pearson knew that, although Canada would continue to be affected by "our old and close association with the United Kingdom ... and, even more, by our growing and sensitive nationalism ...," Canada's most difficult international problems would come from relations with its neighbour, the United States. He noted: "... Canada was more often concerned with carrying out decisions already made by others than with participation in the making of those decisions. We were not consulted about plans and decisions at high levels unless our agreement was essential, and this was seldom."

Pearson's tone with the Americans continued to be informal. That, combined with Pearson's sense of humour and sense of proportion, helped the Canadian legation earn the Americans' trust and confidence. Pearson notes: "While we had our difficulties and differences with the Americans, we were accustomed to discuss and settle them in the frank and outspoken manner which had now become customary between us. We pulled no punches in our official and confidential expression of viewpoints." Articulate, imaginative, and professional, Pearson believed in "quiet diplomacy." "My own experience has been that Canada, in settling her differences and resolving her problems with the United States, usually did better through quiet, rather than headline, diplomacy. Indeed the latter is not diplomacy at all, but international public relations ... [There is a] necessity for quiet and confidential discussion as a prelude to equitable and agreed solutions." Pearson believed that quiet diplomacy, the behind-the-scenes, private give-and-take between diplomats, allowed for more open dialogues and more room for negotiations. Participants felt better able to manoeuvre, investigate possibilities, and try out options if the whole diplomatic process was not always in the public view. Pearson was determined to assist in keeping the channels for communication between nations open.

As a diplomat, Pearson saw his role as shaping the nation, but in addition, he always held onto a broader vision. He saw Canada, not as an isolated country, but as a nation among others, and he was passionate about the need to build a new world order, to connect countries in a meaningful way so they could flourish peacefully. With the end of the war nearing, Pearson became actively involved in the various plans being made for peace. Believing that Canada could help forge strong and peaceful relationships among nations, he continued trying to secure for Canada a voice on the international scene. Pearson's view was that Canada "can most effectively influence international affairs not by aggressive nationalism but by earning the respect of the nations with whom we cooperate, and who will therefore be glad to discuss their international policies with us."

Pearson also began to formulate the view that "power in the conduct of international relations must be related in some way to responsibility. Absolute equality would probably mean absolute futility." This idea, defined by Pearson and a few others, was developed into a principle that became known as "functionalism." Functionalism proposed that a state should have influence on matters proportionate to the degree to which it would be affected. The more directly affected it was, the greater should be the state's influence. Canada was not one of the "Great Powers" and so, Pearson realistically resolved, could not expect an equal hearing or equal involvement on all international matters. But the country was now known as an international "middle power." Was it not logical that it should have a stronger voice in areas that concerned it most?

This view became Canadian foreign policy. It would not be advanced in the now dissolved League of Nations, but in a new forum. Discussions between the British and Americans evolved about the formation of a new body that would be known as the United Nations (UN). The new international organization would fulfill some of the same goals of the League of Nations but have a broader membership. Pearson was keen on the idea, and worked to introduce the concept that the international body would be pro-active, helping to feed a hungry world. In May 1943, when he attended the first formal conference of the UN in West Virginia, it was his suggestion that there be a declaration published to confirm "the determination of the United Nations to deal with the problems of hunger and malnutrition once the war was over."

Following the conference, an Interim Commission was drawn up, consisting of United Nations diplomats in Washington and Pearson as the Canadian representative, to continue sketching out plans for the permanent body. Lester Pearson was nominated chairman of this important committee.

Pearson was raising Canada's profile, but it continued to be a struggle. The United Nations Relief and Rehabilitation Administration (UNRRA) was founded in 1943 as a UN initiative. It was set up to give aid to areas liberated from the Axis powers, which were Germany, Italy, Japan, and their allies. Pearson was involved with the UNRRA and when initially Canada was not to be included on the organization's Central Policy Committee, Pearson wrote: "I warned [Dean Acheson at the American State Department] that if we were refused membership on the Policy Committee of the UNRRA, we might not be able to sign any relief convention."

Finally, with Canada's threat of cutting off financial assistance to Britain, an agreement was reached, but, as Pearson noted, "The Americans should have been more understanding of the Canadian position from the beginning. We were going to be a very important member of the UNRRA and contribute more to its resources than any other country except the United

Pearson presiding at a plenary session of the founding conference of the United Nations Food and Agriculture Organization, 1945

States and the United Kingdom ..." This was "functionalism" in action.

Pearson's role as Canadian representative at UN conferences meeting in the United States was making him a public figure. He became known for his grin, his friendly manner, and his trademark bow tie. The Washington legation had been elevated to an embassy early in 1944, and in January 1945, Pearson was promoted to the position of Ambassador to the United States. He was present with the Canadian delegation as they worked on drafting the UN charter at the founding conference of the UN in San Francisco in April 1945.

Here, the principle of functionalism wasn't as successful for the Canadians. The United States, Britain, the Soviet Union, and China were each given a veto within the UN. (Pearson fought actively against the granting of these vetoes.) Canada believed it had contributed much to the Allied war effort. As a "middle power," it demanded a voice that would carry more weight than the smaller, less involved nations, but it had little success.

Nevertheless, Pearson was encouraged to continue his important work with the UN Commission. Able to mediate between opposing viewpoints and recognized as a shrewd conciliator, Pearson was gaining more and more respect and admiration from his colleagues and peers. He presided over the international conference that met in Quebec in the autumn of 1945 and was successful in drafting a constitution for a UN food and agricultural organization. (The Food and Agricultural Organization was integrated with the United Nations and became the first UN agency.)

Pearson and other Canadian diplomats argued strongly that because Canada was the greatest food producer of the Allies next to the United States, it should have a place on the Combined Food Board set up by Britain and the United States to allocate scarce foodstuffs. Their vigour paid off and Canada won its place on the board. It may, in the end, have been mostly symbolic, but in the world of diplomacy, symbolism is not without importance. Plus, Pearson's determination showed the world that Canada was ready to fight for its rights.

Pearson continued to push Canada forward into engaging actively with the wider world. The war had ended in May 1945 with Germany's capitulation. In August, the United States had dropped atomic bombs on Hiroshima and Nagasaki, and by September, Japan had surrendered. With the end of the war and the threat of atomic weapons looming, Canada could no longer be isolationist—no country could. It had to see itself as part of, and influenced by, the larger world. Pearson himself said: "Everything I learned during the war confirmed and strengthened my view as a Canadian that our foreign policy must not be timid or fearful of commitments but activist in accepting international responsibilities. To me, nationalism and internationalism were two sides of the same coin."

Pearson's work as a peace architect raised his international profile as a Canadian diplomat. He had worked hard, and successfully, to persuade Americans to respond favourably to the idea of an international body, the United Nations, which might actually limit, however slightly, their own independence. He was extraordinarily well informed about Canadian foreign relations, perhaps better than any other Canadian. (Since leaving Canada at age eighteen to fight in the war, he had spent more time outside the country than in it.) In September 1946, Pearson returned to Ottawa where he would serve for two years as under-secretary of state (or deputy minister) for external affairs, the highest position a civil servant could hold.

Louis St. Laurent (left) and William Lyon Mackenzie King at Liberal leadership convention, 1948

Pearson reported directly to King, the prime minister and minister for external affairs, for several months. But King was now seventy-two years old, growing tired, and looking to reduce his workload. As a result, he transferred the position of external affairs over to the minister of justice. This was Louis St. Laurent, a Liberal politician and distinguished

Lester B. Pearson, 1948

Quebec City lawyer.

Pearson respected and admired Louis St. Laurent, and the men shared many views on foreign policy. As deputy minister and minister, the two made a good team. They both had a strong faith in international solutions to problems and believed that Canada must look outwards and become increasingly involved in international organizations. They were united in wanting to support the UN, even though Pearson was beginning to doubt its ability to attain peace among the great powers. They agreed to cooperate as much as possible with the United States and the United Kingdom.

In January 1948, King announced his retirement and persuaded St. Laurent to run as leader of the Liberal party. St. Laurent became prime minister in November 1948. The position of minister for external affairs now had to be filled.

Two years before, King had spoken to Pearson about entering politics, but it was only now that Pearson began to seriously consider it. St. Laurent asked Pearson to replace him as minister for external affairs. This would mean giving up his life in the civil service and entering the political arena.

"As a Minister of External Affairs, I would have far greater responsibility and authority to help determine that Canada's foreign policies were the right ones for the post-war years than I could ever hope to have as a civil servant, no matter how senior I was and however much freedom I was given ... I was now faced with the most difficult decision that I had ever had to make."

After deliberating, Pearson chose to "abandon the professional for the political," and on September 10, 1948, he was appointed secretary of state for external affairs. Because a minister must be a member of one of the Houses of Parliament, Pearson ran in a by-election for the vacated seat in Algoma East riding in Ontario, and on October 25, 1948, he won. On January 26, 1949, Lester Pearson, the man with the bow tie and the grin, entered the House of Commons as a Member of Parliament for the first time.

Chapter 5

The Golden Age of Diplomacy: 1948-1957

Imperialism and Christianity were the supports on which Canada stood as the young Lester Pearson headed off to World War I. Now two world wars were over. Times had changed and traditions had shifted. Pearson began to look to more universal values for more modern times. He advocated tolerance and responsibility. He rejected extremes and instead pursued the "middle way," the compromise. An expert mediator, Pearson was skilled at helping two, or three, sides reach an agreement that, if not pleasing them, did satisfy them.

In addition, Pearson was a firm believer in the goals of the United Nations. But he was also a realist and soon began to accept that the international body had limitations. Throughout Europe and North America, there was concern about the threat of the communist Soviet Union. Although the Soviet Union had fought alongside the Allies against Hitler, the good will toward Russia was beginning to fade. The actions of the Russian representatives at the 1945 UN San Francisco conference were perceived as disruptive and belligerent.

In late 1945, Igor Gouzenko, a cipher clerk at the Soviet embassy in Ottawa, defected and revealed that there had been major Soviet spy rings operating in Canada throughout the war to discover the secret of the atomic bomb. (Canada was involved in atomic research and had, in 1945, opened the new Chalk River atomic centre.) Suspicion and distrust between the Soviets and the West grew. The major powers were

were manoeuvring for control in eastern and central Europe, the Balkans, and Asia, and the Russians began imposing communist governments in Eastern Europe. This was the beginning of the Cold War, a state of hostility between the Soviets and Western nations that lasted decades.

"... [T]he violence of the Cold War [blew] away so many of our earlier hopes and illusions. It was not long, for example, before it became clear that the UN, through the Security Council, could not guarantee the peace and security given priority in the Charter." Pearson's belief echoed that of many others. The UN Security Council had fifteen members, five of which were permanent (including the Soviet Union and the United States) and had a veto. This meant that the "Great Powers" could stand face to face in the Security Council and block any decision-making. Pearson concluded, "Collective security could not, in fact, be organized on a basis of worldwide agreement ... Regional or limited associations for collective defence and security ... might have to be organized."

"Were we to sit and do nothing? ... We must work to strengthen the United Nations as our sole world organization but at the same time build a more limited but firmer structure for collective security, with those countries sharing our views. The North Atlantic seemed the obvious area for such an attempt." Escott Reid of external affairs in Ottawa first advanced the idea in August 1947 of a regional security organization comprised of the peoples of the Western world where the veto would not apply. Now, supported by Louis St. Laurent, Pearson went to Washington to discuss how to achieve a balance of power between the nations. Perhaps Canada and the United States might unite with Western European powers in a North Atlantic alliance. Pearson brought his own hope for a security pact that was more than simply a military guarantee to Europe. It also contained broader positive features embodying western liberal values and greater economic cooperation that would allow the peacekeeping pact to outlive the urgent Soviet threat.

Discussions went on for months with Canada taking a leading role, and on April 4, 1949, the North Atlantic Treaty was signed by Canada, Britain, the United States, and the nations of Western Europe. NATO was formed. Although Pearson's fight for the inclusion of a strong statement of non-military cooperation (Article 2 or "the Canadian Article") eventually ended with a disappointingly watered-down version, he always felt that the formation of NATO was one of the most important things he ever participated in. (Pearson was chairman of the NATO Council from 1951 to 1952 and headed the Canadian delegation to NATO until 1957.)

On June 25, 1950, the Korean War began when the forces of North Korea invaded South Korea. After World War II, Korea was freed from Japanese control and divided into a northern and southern zone. The north was communist, under the control of the Soviet Union, and the south was American-influenced. The Cold War prevented the two zones from merging into one country. When the Northern armies, with arms supplied by China and the Soviet Union, invaded the South, the United Nations Security Council passed a resolution requesting that North Korea halt its aggression. The Americans offered naval and air assistance to South Korea.

Pearson writes: "We felt we should participate as a member of the United Nations but we wanted to be absolutely certain that this would be a United Nations and not a United States operation."

Debates in the Canadian Cabinet culminated in St. Laurent expressing his support for an active Canadian involvement in Korea. Canada easily raised a volunteer brigade of troops to fight in Korea in the name of collective security. An advance battalion

Pearson at the Podium as President of the UN General Assembly, 1952

arrived in December 1950. This was the first stationing abroad of Canadian troops in peacetime. In May 1951 they were joined by the Canadian Army Special Force, created specially for carrying out Canadian obligations under the UN charter or the North Atlantic Pact.

Pearson, uneasy about the American zeal in fighting the war and worried that it would expand into a major war with China, worked to restrain the American decision-makers from risky actions. He and other Canadian diplomats tried to advance arguments for a negotiated peace, for a diplomatic rather than a military solution. Pearson was on a three-person Ceasefire Committee, convened in December 1950. As President of the United

Lester Pearson in Moscow being interviewed by Canadian reporter René Lévesque

Nations General Assembly in 1952, he saw his main task as helping find a solution to the Korean conflict. The effect of this moderating influence remains uncertain. The Americans felt Pearson was too ready to compromise on points of principle. The war ended July 27, 1953, with neither side achieving its goals.

The dictator of the Soviet Union, Josef Stalin, died in March 1953 and was replaced by Nikita Krushchev, who denounced Stalin's crimes and excesses. When invited to visit the Soviet Union in 1955 as minister of external affairs, Pearson did so with hopes of building new bridges between the two countries. The Russian leader condemned NATO, but a Canadian-Russian trade agreement was signed.

The next major diplomatic crisis to involve Pearson was the Suez crisis. Although, through his work in the UN, Pearson had been involved in the creation of the state of Israel in 1947–48, he actually knew very little about the Middle East. In fact, he had only ever travelled to one Middle Eastern country, Egypt, in 1955. The Suez Canal was in Egypt and connected the Mediterranean and Red seas. It had been operated by a British–French company for 85 years when, on July 26, 1956, the Egyptian President Gamal Abdul Nasser seized the company and took over the canal. Only one week before, suspicious of Nasser's growing ties to the Soviet bloc, the United States and Britain had withdrawn their promises of help to finance Egypt's Aswan dam on the Nile River. It seemed that Nasser's bold nationalization of the Suez Canal was an act of retaliation. Britain and France reacted strongly. They feared Western oil supplies moving through the canal were in danger. Both countries viewed Nasser as a dangerous influence on their interests in the Middle East and North Africa. Plus, their national pride was hurt.

Pearson, however, was opposed to Britain trying to regain control over any colonial territory. The British Empire was dead and had been replaced by a Commonwealth of free nations, multi-racial and widely differing, but with some common interests. Pearson worried that any British action in the Suez would cause a rift in the Commonwealth, especially among the Asian members, and would perhaps create animosity between Britain and the United States and indeed within NATO itself. He supported discussion in the UN, however he advised Britain against threatening force against Egypt.

But Britain, France, and Israel were secretly making plans together, and on October 29, Israel attacked Egypt. France and Britain, as privately agreed beforehand with Israel, ordered Israel and Egypt to withdraw from the canal area. Pearson, greatly disturbed, expressed dismay to London that it had acted without authorization by the UN and without consulting allies.

Israel, again as prearranged, accepted the withdrawal ultimatum, but Nasser refused to withdraw. Britain moved swiftly to bomb the Canal Zone, and soon British and French troops were landing in Egypt. The United States and Canada were angry and shocked at the European countries' actions—and yet Ottawa's policy, largely directed by Pearson, was conciliatory. Pearson tried to remain level-headed and seek the best outcome for this volatile situation. He chose to work at helping Britain and France save face, preserving what remained of the NATO alliance, and keeping the Americans talking with the British and French.

On November 2, the UN General Assembly voted in support of resolutions demanding a cease-fire. Canada abstained. The resolution did not have a provision authorizing a UN emergency peace and police force to move in and police the cease-fire and make arrangements for a political settlement. How long could any cease-fire last, Pearson reasoned, without a way to resolve the disagreement?

Pearson hastily pushed ahead with writing a new resolution. He was determined to come up with terms acceptable to the Americans, the British, and the French to limit, if not prevent, the war, and ease the British and French out of Egypt. Pearson spent the day speaking to the Canadian Cabinet and

Canadian members of UNEF on the border between Egypt and Israel

officials in Washington and London, writing, and rewriting, the draft of his plan.

He introduced the new resolution to the Assembly on the night of November 3: "The General Assembly ... requests ... the Secretary General to submit to it within forty-eight hours a plan for the setting up, with the consent of the nations concerned, of an emergency international United Nations force to secure and supervise the cessation of hostilities in accordance with the terms of the above Resolution."

The resolution passed with 19 delegates, including Egypt and Israel, abstaining, but none opposed. A UN Emergency Force (UNEF) had been created, UN peacekeeping was born, and the crisis was averted. Although the idea for the peacekeeping force to separate the combatants was not originally Pearson's, he had been the one to fight for its implementation.

Ironically, when a Canadian battalion was offered to the UNEF, which would be commanded by a Canadian, General E.L.M. Burns, Nasser refused to accept it. He feared the similarity between the British (the aggressors) and Canadians in their uniforms, flags, and language might lead to possible "accidents." Pearson noted: "I considered the Egyptian position outrageous ... Canada, I pointed out, had taken an entirely independent and objective position in the United Nations, not an easy thing to do given our close and friendly association with the British. Having taken this independent position, it would be very hard for Canadians to be told that their troops were not considered independent." He noted that all forces with the UN would be given badges and special pale blue helmets to wear. In the end, Canada supplied administrative personnel instead of infantry, an acceptable compromise to both countries. The cease-fire was achieved on November 6. French and British forces withdrew from Egypt in December, and Israel withdrew in March 1957.

In October 1957, in honour of his work in creating the UNEF and defusing the situation in the Suez, Pearson became the first Canadian to be awarded the Nobel Peace Prize. In his acceptance speech, he stated: "The stark and inescapable fact is that today we cannot defend our society by war since total war is total destruction, and if war is used as an instrument of policy, eventually we will have total war. Therefore, the best defence of peace is not power, but the removal of the causes of war, and international agreements which will put peace on a stronger foundation than the terror of destruction."

Lester Pearson, with Maryon Pearson, shows Nobel Peace Prize

He also summarized another of his strong beliefs in the following statement from his Nobel address: "In his response to the situations he has to meet as a person, the individual accepts the fact that his own single will cannot prevail against that of his group or his society. If he tries to make it prevail against the general will, he will be in trouble. So he compromises and agrees and tolerates. As a result, men normally live together in their own national society without war or chaos. So it must be one day in international society. If there is to be peace, there must be compromise, tolerance, agreement."

Chapter 6
A Losing Leader: 1957-1958

Changes in the international political scene were ending Canada's golden age of diplomacy. There were changes on the home front too. A technological revolution was occurring. Canadian children born in the mid-1950s were born into an age of tape decks and instant foods, supertankers and computers, automatic dishwashers and photocopy machines. They were the first to grow up with television. The whole family could actually watch, on the black-and-white screen in their living room, the first man walking on the moon.

As Pearson would later write in his memoirs: "Today's world will never be as calm and clear as the world of my youth and few can now escape an awareness of what is going on; modern communications bring the world and all its problems and dangers and tragedies right into the living-room."

As well as incredible technological progress, there was increasing national wealth and a general belief that a competent government could positively affect the growth of the national economy. The public had rising expectations of higher standards of living. They were also looking to politicians for strong leadership, for the continuation of the kind of leadership that had taken Canada through the war and post-war years. There was speculation that, if Louis St. Laurent stepped down as leader of the Liberal party, Lester Pearson, the minister for external affairs, might be chosen as the next leader.

Pearson himself, however, likely viewed this possibility with detachment. Although he wasn't completely without ambition, he may have felt guilty about it, and so he tried to hide the unseemly trait. Pearson's own notions of politicians were unflattering, so perhaps it's not remarkable that he didn't consider himself "a really good politician."

Some have said that Pearson actually had an "anti-political" attitude. After all, he had spent most of his adult years in the non-partisan world of the civil service. Even as a minister in foreign affairs, his policies had, for the most part, been "all-party" policies with all parties in basic agreement with them. The Canadian consensus in foreign policy, its emphasis on national-ism, internationalism, and col-lective security, had been labelled "Pearsonian."

Building the trans-Canada pipeline

Now, however, the general shared outlook on issues beyond the national borders was dissolv-ing. In 1956, external matters became a source of conflict between the parties for the first time in many years when an all-Canadian pipeline was debated in Parliament. The idea began with a concern about Canadian control of its resources. Money was pouring into Canada from the United States as American companies hunted for oil and minerals under the Canadian soil. Large reserves of oil and natural gas were found in Alberta, but eastern Canada was using energy supplied from the southern United States.

C.D. Howe, the Liberal minister of defence production and of trade and commerce, was worried about eastern Canada becoming dependent on American energy. Howe made plans for a pipeline that would carry natural gas from Alberta to cen-tral Canada, running entirely within Canada. The pipeline would be primarily privately funded. In 1954, a syndicate was formed that was made up of Canadians and Americans, called TransCanada Pipelines, and for a time there were more Americans than Canadians involved, a fact that would end up causing controversy.

Howe introduced the "pipeline bill" in parliament in May 1956. The bill would authorize the construction of the pipeline and an $80 million loan to the pipeline company from the gov-ernment. The bill had to be approved quickly in order to allow for construction in that same year. Because of the time constraint, Howe put forth a motion for closure (a procedure for ending a debate and taking a vote) to limit the debate.

Knowing the public was increasingly concerned with rising American investment in Canada, the opposition accused the Liberals of pro-Americanism. On the last night of the debate, June 5, 1956, Pearson defended the bill and denied that it was a "sell-out" to American interests. He recalled: "I did not want to take part, but I simply felt I had to ... [T]hat night I became a real tub-thumper. This was the first truly partisan political speech I had made in eight years in the House of Commons, certainly the first outside the arena of foreign affairs." Pearson's speech won him praise from his party.

But the real issue for the opposition became the Liberal party's use of closure. They pounced on it as proof of the government's arrogance.

Pearson recounts: "When [the opposition party] argued bitterly against [Howe] as a dictator, a fascist, and a destroyer of Parliament, when they said that no matter how we did this they were not going to let this bill go through, everything collapsed into complete chaos. It became a wild and irrational struggle, a parliamentary débâcle."

Legislation was passed on June 7, but the damage had been done. The Canadian public saw the Liberal party's call for closure as being tyrannical and reflecting improper parliamentary procedure. The next year an election was called for June 10. Among other factors, the voters were influenced by the government's record on foreign affairs. Many Canadians were proud of Canada's role as peacemaker in the Suez, but there were also many English Canadians who accused Pearson of having betrayed Britain during the Suez crisis. The pro-American, anti-democratic spins put on the pipeline affair harmed the Liberal party in the election.

In addition, it seemed that the Canadian people desperately wanted a change. After all, the Liberal party had been the government for twenty years. Perhaps it was time for a new party and a new leader.

The new Conservative leader, John Diefenbaker, was a 61-year-old lawyer and a veteran Saskatchewan politician. A dynamic speaker and a civil libertarian, Diefenbaker ran under the slogan "Time for a change." And on June 10, 1957, that's what the Canadian people voted for. In a surprise, although narrow, win, the Conservatives defeated the Liberals with 112 seats to 105 seats. (The CCF won 25 seats, Social Credit 19, Independents 2, Independent Liberals 1, and Liberal Labour 1.)

Louis St. Laurent resigned as Liberal leader in September. Pearson wrote: "The pressure grew on me to stand for the leadership and I was caught up in a turmoil of contradictory emotions. I had very real doubts about my fitness for party leadership, for operating successfully the management side of politics, where I had so little experience. My training for political leadership, to say the least, was unusual. A life that had taken me from student to professor to diplomat was a better preparation for government than for politics. I had never anticipated politics as a career ... Despite my doubts about my qualifications, however, it seemed to me that a member of a party who had benefited from the years in power in the sense that he had been given a post of responsibility, authority, and privilege ... had no right to reject the invitation of his friends to allow his name to go before the convention."

John Diefenbaker (left) becomes Conservative party leader in 1956

Pearson, the face of Canada's foreign service and a Nobel prize winner, agreed to become a candidate at the Liberal leadership convention held in January 1958. He handily defeated Paul Martin by 1,084 votes to 305 and became the new Liberal leader.

Pearson stood up to make his first speech as Leader of the Opposition on January 20. It was meant to launch Pearson as the leader of the party. Pearson's speaking style was quite different from Diefenbaker's—it was milder, less blustery, and carried the hint of a stutter—but it was the content of the speech on this day that made it a disaster, as Pearson himself admitted. As suggested to him by "the experts, our professional politicians," Pearson attacked the Conservatives' record, claiming that the Canadian economy had declined since the new government took over. He proposed that only Liberal policies could deal effectively with the country's real problems. Only a few months after the voters had chosen the new government, Pearson was proposing that the government resign. "I have never regretted anything in my political career so much as my proposal that day," he said.

Why? The plan backfired.

Diefenbaker had obtained a secret Liberal document dated March 1957, which was months before the Conservatives took power. The report tracked the growing weakness of the Canadian economy and pointed to further problems. Diefenbaker argued in his typical brilliant and fiery style that the Liberals had known a recession was coming, hadn't acted to prevent it, and were now trying to blame it on the new government. "In the House of Commons the Prime Minister tore me to shreds ... He argued that, as leader of a minority government facing an obstructive opposition, he could not do the exciting things that he had promised in the 1957 campaign and that he must ask the people for a decisive vote of confidence." Pearson's motion that the Conservative government resign was a bust. It was defeated with a vote of 150 to 95.

Diefenbaker seized the moment. He felt that this was the perfect time to consolidate his political position against the arrogant Liberals. Less than two weeks after Pearson's speech, Diefenbaker dissolved Parliament and called a new election for March 31.

"Thus I faced my first campaign as leader," Pearson recounted. "After only a few days to settle into my new responsibilities, I had now to conduct and help organize a national election campaign, about which my experience and knowledge was minimal. No doubt, if we had been ready for the election, the Prime Minister would not have called it."

This time, on March 30, 1958, the Conservatives won 208 out of 265 seats, a majority of the popular vote. Pearson won his seat and continued as Opposition leader—although, as he gloomily noted, "there was hardly a party left to keep liberal."

Chapter 7
Dief the Chief: 1958-1963

The Diefenbaker era had begun—but it wouldn't last long.

"On 12 May 1958 the new Parliament met for the first time ... It was a time for Liberals, after such a defeat and under a new leader—untried—to sit back, be quiet, reasonable, and co-operative; to get busy with the work of regrouping and rebuilding; to be alert but aggressive in opposition; and to see how things developed."

In Pearson's opening speech to Parliament, he attempted to express these views: "We shall try to be guided by something more than mere partisan consideration as we approach our work. While vigorous and alert in carrying out our responsibilities to oppose, we will try to do this in a constructive way and co-operate with the government in all those endeavours which in our view further the national interest."

In part, Pearson's emphasis on cooperation was necessary because the Canadian people had given the Conservatives strong support in the polls and "naturally would be impatient if our government was ... obstructive." But the inclination to be accommodating was also a reflection of Pearson's own leadership style. As noted, some called him "anti-political" because he claimed not to be out to defend or attack a proposal just for political reasons. Pearson did not think in black and white; he was always looking to find something worth agreeing with even in his adversary's position.

Life on Lester Pearson's home front had changed. The Pearsons' children, Geoffrey and Patricia, were away from home and having children of their own. Lester and his wife Maryon were living comfortably in Stornoway, the Opposition leader's residence in Ottawa. "The five years in opposition were, strangely enough, a most productive, rewarding, and stimulating time," Pearson remembered. This might seem to

The Pearsons at Stornoway, official residence of the Opposition leader

be an odd comment, given that the Conservative victory had been stunning, the largest majority in Canadian history to that time, and that the Conservative government went on to successfully implement many popular policies. For example, John Diefenbaker's party addressed the decreasing sales of wheat from the Prairie provinces to Europe by helping stimulate the sale of Canadian wheat to China and the Soviet Union, and it created special funding programs for farmers.

But in general, the Conservative party's years in power would be filled with difficulties. For economic reasons, the government cancelled the development and production of the CF-105 Avro Arrow, a Canadian fighter-interceptor aircraft. As well as eliminating thousands of jobs, this controversial decision also struck a blow to national pride—and provided the Liberal party with a clear platform for an attack. Pearson expressed his opinion this way: "There were reasons of defence and economics that could have been advanced to justify this decision but none to justify the way it was done. Suddenly, on February 20, 1959, without any effort to keep together the fine professional team of scientists and engineers which had been assembled, Mr. Diefenbaker pronounced his government's policy. There was even an apparent vindictiveness in the decision to scrap the five completed planes and the others half completed so that no museum of science and technology would ever be able to show what we could design and produce. It was on this irrational element in the decision that we centred our attack, thus reflecting the feelings of most Canadians."

Although Diefenbaker campaigned to open up the North, he did little about developing northern resources. "Dief the Chief" also alienated French-speaking Canadians and did little to try to understand Quebec's evolving sense of itself as a nation within a nation.

The government's biggest problem, however, was Canada's deteriorating economic situation. Diefenbaker promised to end unemployment and regional disparities, but the post-war economic boom had ended and unemployment was on the rise. Transfer payments to the Maritimes, where incomes were consistently below the national average, increased per capita income only slightly. A severe recession hit in 1960–1961 and, although not the fault of the Conservatives, it limited their ability to suggest, and fund, new development proposals. On the contrary, Canadians had to tighten their belts and the government itself was forced to borrow money from the International Monetary Fund.

A federal election was held on June 19, 1962, and this time, Pearson's "handlers" consulted public-opinion polls to shape Pearson's image. His trademark bow tie was out—a straight tie was in. Although engaging and charming when meeting with individuals, Pearson didn't seem to do well on television or in crowds. In fact, many Canadians viewed him as a "smart-aleck." Perhaps minimizing his jerky arm movements and foregoing his sheepish smile after comments that weren't humorous might help. His speechwriters were instructed to avoid long sentences and words that accentuated Pearson's lisp. Realizing Pearson's "nice guy" personality wasn't going to ignite the voters, new image or not, his advisers pragmatically tried to turn the campaign focus away from the leader and point it more broadly at the whole Pearson team.

Nevertheless, despite grooming tactics, the Conservative party again won. When Pearson telephoned his mother to tell her that he would not be prime minister, her response was cheerful. "She expressed no great distress over this and said: 'Well, I've been watching the campaign and there seems to have been an awful lot of talk about the dollar and financial matters and all that kind of thing, and I notice you've been taking part in these discussions and I was thinking, you know, that perhaps it's just as well that you haven't been asked to take on the Prime Minister's job at this time because you were never very good in arithmetic.'"

Diefenbaker lost his majority, however, and this was a crushing blow to the Conservatives. Pearson was intent on uniting his party toward one goal—bringing down the minority government as soon as possible and winning the next election.

Pearson had two political subjects on his mind, both of which helped bring matters to a head. "Now was the time to do something about them. The first and foremost problem the country faced was national unity; more particularly, the relations between the two founding language groups in our federal structure. Strains had been increasing since 1960 as a result of Jean

Jean Lesage

Lesage's 'Quiet Revolution' and the reluctance of much of English-speaking Canada to respond in a constructive and understanding way to that revolution."

In December 1962, Pearson made a non-partisan speech advocating a Royal Commission on the question of bilingualism and biculturalism as the official recognized basis for Canada's national development. The speech was a hit in French Canada. Both the Liberals and the Conservatives had lost seats in Quebec to the Social Credit party. Pearson hoped that now Quebec would begin looking more favourably toward the Liberal party.

As uninterested as he was in economic matters, Pearson was extremely concerned with nuclear diplomacy in the late 1950s and early 1960s. "The other subject on my mind was national defence and the tragic confusion government policies had created. This was especially so on the question of nuclear weapons; Canada's position was intolerable, or rather the fact that we had no position was intolerable," he wrote.

In 1957, Diefenbaker, on the advice of the Canadian military, had hastily committed Canada to the North American Air Defence Command (NORAD). This agreement integrated the air-defence forces of Canada (the Royal Canadian Air Force) and the United States under a joint command for the purpose of defending the continent. The commander would be American; the second-in-command Canadian.

After the production of the Avro Arrow was cancelled in 1959, Diefenbaker agreed to two things: he agreed to provide Canada's CF-104s in Europe with nuclear weapons, and he agreed to accept American-made Bomarc anti-aircraft missiles at two Canadian bases. In order to be used for the defence of central Canada and the United States against Soviet bombers, the Bomarcs were supposed to be equipped with nuclear warheads and Diefenbaker indicated that these would be obtained. But by the time the missile sites were almost completed, in 1962, Diefenbaker changed his mind. In the midst of great political debate and discussion about nuclear war within the Cabinet and the media, he refused to install nuclear warheads on the Bomarcs.

Then, in the fall of 1962, the Americans discovered that the Soviet Union had installed nuclear missiles in Cuba. Without consulting Canada, they immediately went on standby alert, determined to blockade Cuba until the missiles were removed. The Americans assumed the Canadian government would do likewise, but Diefenbaker delayed putting the Canadian component of NORAD on alert. This failure to back them angered the Americans, the military, and most Canadians. It was the defence minister Douglas Harkness, who, on his own, after two days, eventually gave the order for the Canadian air force to go on alert—even though, without the nuclear warheads, the anti-aircraft missiles were useless.

Pearson and his wife had both been opponents of nuclear weapons until this point. But in late 1962, Paul Hellyer, the Liberal defence critic in the House of Commons, advised Pearson that the Liberal party should change its policies and live up to its commitments to the United States and Europe. After much thought, Pearson changed his mind. "We had taken on obligations ... I judged, as the leader of my party and in the light of changing circumstances, that a Liberal government would discharge the commitments regarding nuclear weapons accepted by Canada under NATO and NORAD."

A Gallup poll showed that most Canadians agreed with Pearson. "That done, we would then begin to negotiate Canada into more appropriate roles, ones which would not require Canadian forces to use nuclear weapons. In contrast with Mr. Diefenbaker's position, mine was at least a decision."

Within the Conservative Cabinet, there was continued disagreement about the issue, and, eventually, even conflicting public statements. The American president, John F. Kennedy, had never tried to hide his dislike of Diefenbaker, and in January 1963, his *The Diefendollar* government issued a harsh press release accusing the Canadian government of not fulfilling its international obligations. On February 4, Defence Minister Harkness resigned from the Conservative cabinet over the nuclear issue. That same day, Pearson moved in the House of Commons that parliament be dis-

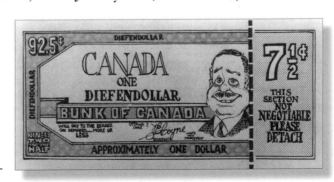

Judy LaMarsh

solved, and the government fell. A new election was called for April 8, 1963.

Once more Diefenbaker and Pearson took to the election trail, criss-crossing the country, shaking hands and making speeches. Some predicted that winning the election would be a walk in the park for the Liberal party, but instead, things went seriously wrong. Several gimmicks were used during the campaign—and back-fired. Colouring books that ridiculed the Conservatives also offended the public, and homing pigeons that were let loose to precede Pearson's arrival never arrived. Judy LaMarsh, the Liberal MP for Niagara Falls, was assigned to be "the Truth Squad"; she would follow Diefenbaker on the campaign trail, take note of any wild and outlandish statements he made, and then point out his lies afterwards. But Diefenbaker turned the tables on the game, introducing LaMarsh at each meeting, providing her with a prominent seat at the table, and then making witty remarks about her.

When the Liberal lead dropped, a new campaign strategy was suggested. Pearson was stating the need for his party to win a clear majority. A minority government, with more seats and votes than any of the other individual parties in the House, still does not have enough to win a vote alone. Thus it is vulnerable, needing support from others in the House. But this appeal to the public for a majority government was coming across as dry and unexciting. Now Pearson de-emphasized this aspect of the campaign and even the Liberal policies themselves. He became an advocate simply for action. And in the last two weeks of the campaign, to really bring home his intentions, Pearson promised "sixty days of decision." The first sixty days that his government was in power would be full of decision-making and action. He pledged to avoid the ho-humming and ineptitude of the Conservative government and move decisively to get things done.

On April 8, 1963, although the Conservatives swept the Prairies and held most of their seats in the Atlantic provinces, the Liberal government was voted in, winning 128 seats. It wasn't a majority, as Pearson had hoped, but it was enough to put the Liberals back in the driver's seat. On April 22, one day before his sixty-sixth birthday, Lester Pearson took office as Canada's four-teenth prime minister.

Chapter 8
Prime Minister Pearson

Lester Pearson took office full of political confidence and optimism. He wrote in a letter to his son Geoffrey, "... [O]ne thing I know, that I am going to be happier, more comfortable and more effective in government—than ever I was in opposition ... I feel fine, full of energy and without any need of a holiday."

Pearson had promised sixty days of action, so he felt pressure to dive right in and start making things happen. The Liberal party already had a rostrum of policies that the candidates had pledged to pursue after the election. These policies arose from a conference held in Kingston, Ontario, in 1960. Spearheaded by Pearson and organized by his trusted left-leaning advisors, it was attended by academics, journalists, and liberal thinkers.

Although the conference was billed as non-partisan, Pearson nonetheless hoped it might breath new life into the Liberal party and help it branch out in new directions. He wanted to rebuild the party, leave behind the policies of the last Liberal government, and come up with new ideas for social policy. "My desire was to forget about the old party, to stop looking to the past ... Most of our recruits were what I would call progressive ... I had begun in 1958 to create a small but excellent staff of advisers ... In the terminology of 1960, they would have been regarded as left-wing Liberals."

Listening to the recommendations of many of the conference speakers, such as Tom Kent, Pearson increasingly became convinced that a wide-ranging program of social reform, including extending economic assistance to the underprivileged in areas such as education, old age assistance, and health, was essential. His interest in social policy initiatives was supported by the delegates to the Liberal National Rally, which was held in January 1961 and chaired by Walter Gordon, a long-time friend of Pearson's. At the rally, the reform policies introduced at the Kingston conference were discussed and voted on. A commitment was made to regional development funds, greater unemployment insurance, limits on foreign control of the Canadian economy, complete processing of raw materials in Canada, health insurance, pension reform, and a Canadian flag, among other things.

Before Parliament assembled, the new prime minister had to choose which ministers to put in place in his new Cabinet. (The Cabinet is the executive committee of the federal government. Its members, called "ministers," are chosen by the prime minister from members of the majority party in the House of Commons.) Pearson did this carefully, regarding it as a "complicated task," as he tried to give representation to each province, with a certain number of ministers from Ontario balanced by a certain number from Quebec, at least one woman, and one or more representatives of the ethnic communities. Of course, he considered many of the people who had helped him during his campaign and stood by him in the opposition government. Some of the choices he made were Paul Martin as the minister of external affairs, Paul Hellyer as defence minister, and Walter Gordon as finance minister. Judy LaMarsh, the only woman in the cabinet, was given the ministry of health and welfare. (When Pauline Jewett asked to be in the cabinet, Pearson turned her down, telling her there was already one woman.)

The Cabinet chosen, Pearson felt it vital that he attend to some of Canada's international relationships. He believed that Diefenbaker had damaged Canada's relationships with Britain and the United States, so on April 30, Pearson spent five days in London, visiting the British prime minister, Harold Macmillan, and members of his Cabinet, as well as the Queen. Shortly after, he spent two days with President John F. Kennedy in Hyannisport, Massachusetts.

"This trip, as that to London, was not meant to establish anything beyond a good personal relationship, and in this it succeeded," Pearson recalled. (He also managed to impress the President with his knowledge of baseball statistics.)

Parliament resumed in mid-May. The Liberals had made the "sixty days" campaign promise in part to prove that they were determined, decisive, and active, not a government of the cautious and elderly. In the spirit of this—although Pearson later admitted more time was needed and should have been taken—

June 13 was fixed as the date for Finance Minister Walter Gordon to present the Liberals' first budget. But Gordon felt that his own deputy minister (who was his right-hand senior civil servant) was inadequate, and his assistant deputies didn't agree with his economic goals. As he raced to prepare the budget, Gordon decided he needed outside help. He hired three technical financial experts from outside the government.

A week before the budget went to Cabinet, Gordon showed the draft budget to Pearson. Although he probably had little understanding of the economic aspects of the budget, and even less interest in it, the prime minister was troubled by one or two of the provisions. He suggested that they go over the draft budget with the Governor of the Bank of Canada, Louis Rasminsky. When the three men met, Rasminsky was in basic agreement with the proposed deficit and agreed that the essential task was to keep the economy expanding to combat the country's high unemployment. Three proposed tax measures worried him immensely, one of which also concerned Pearson. This was the proposed 30 per cent tax on certain foreign takeovers, designed to limit American influence on the Canadian economy. But Rasminsky did not advise extreme caution about the changes, and they remained in the budget.

Walter Gordon

Gordon presented the budget to the House on June 13. The very next day the Opposition let fly. They accused the government of acting in a sinister way by hiring outside experts to help with the budget. Then, a week later, the tax changes were attacked—by the Conservatives, by business, and by the financial media. "Seldom has a budget been so universally condemned, with the thrust of the attack against the tax designed to protect us from American takeovers. It was not the purpose that was attacked but the amount of the tax, which was castigated as impracticable and unfairly discriminating. I do not think I have ever known in my years in Ottawa anything quite so violent and so bitterly hostile to a particular clause in any budget," Pearson wrote.

Gordon offered his resignation, but instead of accepting it, Pearson asked him if he had enough confidence in himself to continue. Gordon said he did, so Pearson encouraged him to stay on as finance minister. But because his was a minority government, Pearson realized they would have to withdraw the budget or modify it—or risk it not passing in the House. As Pearson pragmatically noted, "almost instinctively and unconsciously a minority government looks for legislation likely to get at least some support from the other parties because, naturally, if that support is not given, defeat and an election will result."

Gordon revised much of the budget, and this early embarrassing fiasco shook the Liberals. They had campaigned to bring efficiency and action to government, but now they had to revise, and delay implementation, of their very first budget.

Still, the pressure was on to keep the momentum going. In July 1963, Pearson moved quickly to fulfill one of his election promises to address the changing aspirations of Quebec. He appointed the Royal Commission on Bilingualism and Biculturalism with the goal of studying, not only language rights, but also Quebec's place in Canada as a distinct society. Quebec had recently leapt into the modern age, turning from a rural society into an urban, industrial society almost overnight. Many French Canadians began rejecting the past, questioning tradition, and challenging authority. They made new demands on Ottawa and questioned the notion of federalism. More and more French Canadians supported separatism. The Liberals had won the 1960 provincial election in Quebec under Jean Lesage, who campaigned with the slogan "Maîtres chez nous" or "Masters in our own house." Lesage's government was actively seeking change.

Pearson himself was extremely interested in Quebec's challenge to Canadian federalism. He believed in the equality of French- and English-speaking Canadians and maintained that Canada's two founding peoples were partners—equal partners. He was passionately committed to the unity of Canada, but Pearson had changed his views about a strong central government. He now was supportive of the idea of strong provincial governments, optimistic that this was the best way to keep the country unified.

Instead of Ottawa leading the way, which was something he knew Quebec would not tolerate, the approach he now chose was a "cooperative federalism." This reflected something of his own personal style; he sought consensus and a common purpose. Cooperative federalism would mean more financial independence and more decision-making for the provinces. It would require negotiations and compromises. (There had been only 7 federal-provincial meetings in 1939. There would be 125 in 1965.) It would actually mean a new way of working. With the Pearson government, federal-provincial diplomacy became the Canadian way.

Also with Quebec's interests in mind, Pearson appointed seven francophones from that province and three from other provinces to his Cabinet. The Pearson Cabinet thus had more francophones than any other Cabinet in Canadian history.

In addition, Pearson promised to try to find a way to accommodate Quebec's refusal to participate in various federal programs. This first came to a head during discussions about the Canada Pension Plan. Because of improved health care, more Canadians were living longer. During his campaign, Pearson promised that, immediately upon election, he would assist the aging population by putting into place a national pension plan. Individuals and employers would contribute to a universal fund, and after the age of 65, the contributors, or their widow/ers or dependents, could draw from this pool of money.

On the sixtieth "day of decision," the Canada Pension Plan resolution was announced. Discussions with the provinces began soon after, and slowly, one after another, the provinces came on board and agreed to the financial assistance—all except Quebec, that is. The Quebec government saw the federal plan as a threat to its provincial autonomy and thus to its cultural survival.

A huge battle ensued between Ottawa and Quebec. Finally, a deal was reached. Quebec got its own Quebec Pension Plan, which was separate from, but parallel to, the federal government's plan for the other provinces, the Canada Pension Plan.

Some Canadians feared such measures might threaten the unity of the country. On the other hand, many nationalists in Quebec didn't think Pearson was doing enough to accommodate their needs. Overall, there was no consensus among Canadians about Quebec. It is not surprising, then, that, as unrest in Quebec grew, everyone seemed dissatisfied with the leader's efforts.

Pearson was a believer in the liberal principle of equality of opportunity and so he encouraged his ministers to quickly begin putting into place the many other social policies it had promised. Neither interested nor comfortable giving detailed advice in the areas of either economics or social policy, the prime minister was happy to delegate this work to other ministers and remain involved in only a general way.

Under the Canada Assistance Plan of 1965, the government agreed to share the costs (with provincial and municipal governments) of a broad spectrum of welfare administration and income support programs, such as mothers' allowances, health care for the needy, and child care. The Liberal government was also determined to protect individuals against rising medical costs. In 1965 it introduced a comprehensive medical insurance scheme. The plan was based on a set of principles upholding equal access and set out in national legislation. All the provinces, even Quebec, had to conform to these principles. Pearson announced Medicare in 1965; it came into effect in 1968. "I regarded it as a major triumph," noted Pearson in his memoirs. "By that time I had left office, but I could still look back in pride." Now sickness and medical emergencies would not empty the bank accounts of Canadian families.

Then in June 1964, Pearson proposed a resolution in Parliament providing for a distinctive national flag. Until then, the British flag had flown over Canada. "For me, the flag was part of a deliberate design to strengthen national unity, to improve federal-provincial relations, to devise a more appropriate constitution, and to guard against the wrong kind of American penetration. It was our purpose to develop national symbols which would give us pride and confidence and belief in Canada," recalled Pearson.

He presented his choice of flag to Parliament, a white flag with three red maple leaves in the centre and a

Supporters of the Red Ensign parade on Parliament Hill

vertical wavy blue band on each edge that became known as the "Pearson pennant." A huge debate ensued that went on ... and on ... and on for six and a half weeks of parliamentary time. Public opinion seemed split. Diefenbaker and many Conservatives argued that tradition was being threatened and that the new flag, any new flag, was a betrayal of Canada's longstanding and important connection to Britain. Diefenbaker refused to compromise and give up the flag that had, for decades, flown over Canada, the British Red Ensign. Others refused the idea of a new flag because they saw it as one more appeasement to Quebec. Still others clearly wanted a "distinctive Canadian flag" of some design that celebrated their nation.

Finally, on December 11, closure was introduced to end the weeks of debate. (This was the same procedure that had been called for by Howe during the pipeline debate.) Members of the House voted, and on December 13, the maple leaf flag, a red maple leaf on a white background with two red bars on each side, was adopted. Canadians had their own symbol for their own nation. Lester Pearson, the champion of the national flag, was thrilled.

Despite all these many legislative successes, there were troubles in Pearson's government, too. Terrible scandals and allegations of corruption and personal dishonesty abounded in 1964 and early 1965, many of them involving the Liberals' Quebec ministers. Parliament became bogged down in hours

Members of Parliament hold up the new Canadian flag

and hours of bitter personal disputes that had nothing to do with government policies. The Canadian people began questioning the prime minister's ability to lead. It was only a matter of time before the inevitable happened.

Chapter 9
The Second Term

"One of my most important political decisions as Prime Minister was to hold a general election in 1965. We had been having a rough time as a minority facing a difficult Parliament. A vigorous, almost violent Opposition was cutting us down on every possible occasion and making our lives very uncomfortable."

Hoping to win a majority government, Pearson faced off against Diefenbaker one more time, but, on November 7, 1965, once again, the Liberals succeeded in winning only a minority government. "My own first reaction was to resign the leadership. This was partly a reaction of disappointment but, more than that, I wanted to leave … I had had enough, and would have been very happy to drop out."

Pearson offered his resignation to the Cabinet when it first met on November 10, but it was refused. Pearson would carry on as prime minister for three more years.

The first thing Pearson did was build a new team. He reorganized his Cabinet, bringing in new ministers and transferring others into new jobs. Finance Minister Walter Gordon, who was also chairman of the Liberal party organization, resigned from the Cabinet, penitent for having urged Pearson to call the election. Pearson replaced him with the cautious Mitchell Sharp, who spoke against measures to curb foreign investment. Sharp was eventually replaced with Robert Winters, who was known to be very critical of Gordon's views. Jean Marchand, Gérard Pelletier, and Pierre Trudeau, newly elected in Quebec in 1965 and strong federalists, quickly became prominent in the Cabinet.

Pearson's government continued to pursue issues of justice and equality. In 1966 the first serious discussion of the abolition of the death penalty took place in the House of Commons. Although the Liberal motion for abolition was rejected at that time, the next year Pearson succeeded in passing legislation that suspended the death penalty for all crimes of murder except the killing of a police officer or a prison guard in the execution of their duties. (When this moratorium on the death penalty ended five years later, it was extended for an additional five years. Before this time elapsed, Pierre Trudeau's government introduced, and saw passed on July 26, 1976, Bill C-84, which abolished the death penalty.)

Also in 1967, at the urging of women's groups, ministers such as Judy LaMarsh, and Pearson's wife Maryon, Prime Minister Pearson created the Royal Commission on the Status of Women. The commission held public hearings in fourteen cities and visited every Canadian province and territory. Its report, completed in 1970, made 167 recommendations, including equal pay for work of equal value, paid maternity leave, and a national day-care network.

Nationalism was still the buzzword of the 1960s. One of Pearson's major goals was to change the Canadian constitution— still a statute of the British Parliament—to make it relevant to an independent Canada. The St. Laurent government had succeeded in gaining the ability to amend the sections of the British North America Act that applied to the federal government alone. But whenever Parliament wanted any other parts of the constitution amended, it had to ask the British Parliament to do it. Pearson wanted an amending formula that would allow all sections of the Canadian constitution to be amended in Canada.

In 1964, an amending procedure called the Fulton–Favreau formula was proposed at a federal-provincial meeting at Charlottetown, but not agreed to by all parties. Pearson made many concessions in other areas, hoping to win Quebec's support for the Fulton–Favreau formula, and at first, this was successful. But then the progress began to deteriorate. The Federal–Provincial Constitutional Conference in February 1968 brought no deal to the table between the provinces and Ottawa. Canadians would have to wait for another government, one led by Pierre Trudeau, before Canada's constitution would be patriated.

Canada was still being challenged by the United States—economically and politically. Canadian nationalists feared that Canada was being Americanized and that Pearson was doing little to stop it. After their initial budget failure in 1963, the Liberals backed away from trying to control American investments in Canada. Then in 1965, the Liberals introduced legislation to

Canadians protesting the war in Vietnam

assist Canadian magazines; it disallowed income tax deductions for advertising in non-Canadian publications. The hope was that this would reduce the distribution of American journals in Canada. But the United States protested and Pearson backed down, allowing exemptions for the two biggest American magazines in Canada, *Time* and *Reader's Digest*.

Then the Liberals negotiated the Canada–U.S. Autopact of 1965 with the United States. This agreement closely integrated the automotive industry, establishing free trade on the continent in automobiles and parts. (Canada agreed to produce only as much as it could sell.) The Canadian economy benefited, but nationalists protested that Canada was becoming tied more closely to the American economy.

On the political front, Pearson and President Lyndon Johnson were practising "quiet diplomacy." Any disagreement or debating was done in private. The public saw a generally united front expressing shared views. But in April 1965, this changed.

The United States was increasingly involved in the war in Vietnam. It allied itself with South Vietnam against the North Vietnamese, and engaged in a massive bombing of North Vietnam. Deliberately kept in the dark about the American plans, Pearson was concerned about the escalation of the war and decided to speak out directly. He provoked the anger of President Lyndon Johnson when he made a speech in Philadelphia urging the United States to stop bombing and work toward a peaceful solution to the war. At a subsequent meeting with Pearson, a furious Johnson actually grabbed the Canadian prime minister by the shirt and reprimanded him.

Pearson remained critical of American actions in Vietnam for a time, speaking privately to Johnson when he came to Expo in 1967 and again urging that the bombing be stopped, but it became clear that he was unable to influence the President. Canadian–American relations had shifted.

Pearson still remained very much committed to the international institutions, but again, times were changing. Paul Martin, Canada's external affairs minister, made a speech at the United Nations in September calling for an unconditional halt to the bombing in Vietnam, but the United Nations, the institution that had once been the instrument for Canada's voice, was now being ignored by the participants in the Vietnam war.

And the Commonwealth, that other forum that Pearson championed? When Rhodesia declared independence from Britain, Pearson shone as a mediator between the British and black African Commonwealth members at the 1966 Commonwealth meetings, eventually helping reach a compromise. Pearson recognized the changing face of the organization, and, although it was gradually declining in importance, he continued to value it enormously. "We are no longer trying to claim that the Commonwealth is a political entity ... While there is no constitutional or legal relationship among its members, there is a social, even a family, relationship which persists ... It is, if I may use the word, a fellowship, the great value of which stems from the fact that it is an association of peoples of every race, freely joined together as equals in the hope that they have something to offer one another and can give the world an example of interracial as well as international friendship and co-operation."

Charles de Gaulle visits Montreal

The highlight of Pearson's final term as prime minister was the celebration of Canada's centennial in 1967. Expo '67 in Montreal was like a big national birthday party, enthusiastic, vibrant, and fun. Yet despite its success as a national endeavour, Canadians were overwhelmed by the huge cost of the event. They were experiencing a growing sense that there had to be limits imposed on government spending.

Also, Expo '67 highlighted the Quebec conflict once more. Pearson's own view of Quebec's place in Canada never wavered, but there was an increasing divide between Ottawa and Quebec. And the public's view of Pearson's strategies remained divided. Diefenbaker accused him of always doing

*Pierre Elliott Trudeau
becomes Pearson's successor*

too much, of always giving in to Quebec. The French-Canadians always seemed to accuse him of not doing enough.

But when, in 1967, the French President General de Gaulle visited Montreal and, from the balcony of the city hall, cried to the crowd: "Vive le Québec libre" (the separatist slogan), a furious Pearson acted quickly and decisively. He recalled, "I could hardly believe my ears ... This was the slogan of separatists dedicated to the dismemberment of that Canada whose independence de Gaulle had wished to see assured only a few years before ... This was a reflection on and almost an insult to the federal government." Pearson prepared a statement and read it on the radio the next evening. He called de Gaulle's words "unacceptable." He emphasized that all the people in every province of Canada are free and did not need to be liberated. He promised that "Canada will remain united and will reject any effort to destroy her unity." De Gaulle left Canada the next day.

Canadians still very much admired Pearson, but there seemed to be a lack of team spirit among his Cabinet members. Pearson was accused of being unable to lead. He was accused of always telling people what they wanted to hear—and then not necessarily following through on what they expected him to do. In fact, the public was becoming cynical about the leaders of both the government and the Opposition. Mud-slinging and improprieties seemed to constantly preoccupy the House.

The public yearned for a new type of leadership, one that was dynamic and imaginative, one that could do away with finger-pointing and name-calling. Diefenbaker was replaced as leader of the Conservative party by Robert Stanfield in September 1967 and, at the end of the Centennial year, on December 14, 1967, Pearson announced his resignation. "I had a great sense of relief, of course, and at the same time a natural feeling of sadness at giving up my political career and the responsibility of the office; but the overriding emotion was still one of relief ... The 23rd of April 1967 was my seventieth birthday. My wife and I had discussed our future and I had already decided to retire in my seventieth year. I would have done so that April had it not been Canada's Centennial year."

In 1968, Pierre Trudeau, the intelligent forty-eight-year-old swinging bachelor and former minister of justice, was chosen as the new Liberal leader and Lester Pearson's successor.

That same year, Pearson headed up a Commission on International Development for the World Bank. Its goal was to study the impact of several decades of international aid on the underdeveloped world. The commission's report, published in October 1969, recommended increasing international aid and encouraging partnerships between donor and recipient countries.

Pearson began teaching at Carleton University in 1969 and writing his memoirs. (There would be three volumes. Most of the Pearson quotes in this book are from these published memoirs.) He also became honorary chairman of Canada's first major league baseball team, the Montreal Expos. And he loved being able to spend more time playing with his grandchildren.

But sadly, Pearson's health was soon in jeopardy. A benign growth near his ear had been removed in 1963. In 1970, the cancer was back and he lost an eye to it. The cancer was spreading, but Pearson continued to teach, to promote his books, and to keep a busy schedule. His health began to fade again in October. While in Florida on vacation in December 1972, Pearson col-

Lester B. Pearson lying in state, December 1972

lapsed. The cancer had spread to his liver.

Pearson was flown home to Ottawa on Christmas Eve and fell into a coma on December 27, 1972. He died with his wife and two children at his bedside. On December 31, Lester Pearson was buried in a little cemetery in the Gatineau Hills, north of Ottawa.

Chapter 10
Pearson's Legacy

S ay the name "Lester Pearson" to a Canadian and ask what it means to him or her. Many will remember Pearson the man and his great personal charm. Pearson may not have been a fabulous speaker or a terrific administrator, but he was witty and warm. He was loveable. Pearson was also understanding and receptive, important qualities for a negotiator and diplomat. But, interestingly, no matter how accessible people found him, no matter how open he always was to hearing what they had to say, Lester Pearson was also described as elusive. Many people, even those closest to him, believed they never really knew the inner Lester Pearson. He revealed only so much, keeping his secret self buried away.

Again, say "Lester Pearson" to a Canadian and many will think of Pearson's success as prime minister in bringing Canada its maple leaf flag. Many will note the many supportive social policies introduced by his government to benefit the unemployed, the weak, the poor, the disadvantaged. There may even be mention of his trademark bow tie, his lisp, and his mild-mannered style. Certainly, the image of Pearson as prime minister was never one of a dynamic spotlight-grabbing leader.

Pearson himself understood and accepted that there were different styles of leadership. He was not one to hold the reins tightly and control those around him. Rather, as he wrote, "more often, from my own experience, it is preferable to exercise a loose and flexible control, to rely on consensus rather than on compulsion, except in those rare circumstances when one man must act, and act quickly. I do have a weakness or a strength, whichever way you look at it (and that is perhaps one reason why I first went into the diplomatic service), of examining every side of a question before coming to a decision."

Pearson preferred to discuss, argue, come to an agreement, and then link arms and walk side-by-side with others. It usually took longer to reach a decision this way. It wasn't as flashy. But it was the Pearson way. Not all Canadians liked it. Those surveyed before his last election in 1965 complained that Pearson wasn't aggressive enough. They pointed out that he wasn't doing a great job. But, on the other hand, those surveyed didn't think he was doing a bad job either. The voters believed that Pearson was honest. They believed that he was trying hard.

Say the name "Lester Pearson" to a Canadian and ask what it means to him or her. Many will remember him for toppling popular John Diefenbaker from power. Many will remember him for rebuilding the Liberal party. Without question, a vast number of Canadians will proudly remember Lester Pearson as one of the great diplomats of his time and winner of the Nobel Peace Prize. It is his work as Canada's representative in the world of foreign affairs that has left Canada an intellectual and moral legacy. His philosophy and style, which became known as "Pearsonian diplomacy," reflected his vision of how Canada should be and how Canada should behave.

Pearson saw Canada's role as honest broker and helpful fixer, builder of institutions, negotiator, peacekeeper, donor, humanitarian. Representing Canada on the world stage, he embodied and cultivated these values. His values became Canadian values, and this vision of Canada, so strong and so broad in its appeal, became a mirror in which Canadians could view themselves. It became a shared vision, and also a standard against which they could measure themselves, a standard they could strive to attain.

Pearsonian principles of foreign policy touched such a chord with Canadians that, in a real sense, they still exist today. Successive governments have gone on to maintain and implement these same principles. Canada has an international reputation as a peacekeeper and a friend to nations in need.

Pearson, however, would be the first to caution that Canada not rest on its laurels but continue to remain active and accept responsibility. He knew that a great country does more than look after itself. It goes beyond doing only what it should do. Pearson knew that Canada could be better, and he worked to make it so. What he leaves behind is the inspiration for Canadians to imagine what Canada might do—and to work to make it so.

Lester B. Pearson

1897	Lester Bowles Pearson is born on April 23 in Newtonbrook, Ontario
1913	Graduates from Hamilton Collegiate Institute
1914	England and the British Empire declare war on Germany on August 4
1915	Signs up with University of Toronto Hospital Unit and is sent to England
1917	Transfers to the Royal Flying Corps (RFC); hit by a bus in London
1918	Suffers a nervous breakdown
1919	Graduates from University of Toronto
1921	Begins history studies at Oxford University in England
1923	Becomes history lecturer at University of Toronto
1925	Marries Maryon Moody
1928	Joins Department of External Affairs as First Secretary
1935	Transferred to the Canadian High Commission in London, England
1939	Canada declares war on Germany on September 10
1941	Returns to Ottawa
1942	Sent to Washington for duration of war
1945	Becomes Ambassador to the United States
1946	Returns to Ottawa and becomes deputy minister for external affairs
1948	Becomes minister for external affairs
	Elected Member of Parliament for Algoma East riding
1952	Becomes President of UN General Assembly
1957	Wins Nobel Peace Prize for his role in settling the Suez Crisis
1958	Becomes leader of the Liberal Party
1963	Elected Canada's 14th prime minister with a minority government
1965	Wins second election with minority government
1967	Resigns as prime minister
1972	Dies of cancer and is buried on December 31

Further Reading

Bothwell, Robert. *Pearson: His Life and World.* Toronto: McGraw Hill Ryerson Limited, 1978.

English, John. *Shadow of Heaven: The Life of Lester Pearson Volume One: 1897-1948.* Toronto: Lester & Orpen Dennys, 1989; and *The World Years: The Life of Lester Pearson Volume Two: 1949-1972.* Albert A. Knopf, 1992.

Hillmer, Norman, ed. *Pearson, The Unlikely Gladiator.* Montreal and Kingston: McGill-Queen's University Press, 1999.

Pearson, Geoffrey. *Seize the Day: Lester B. Pearson and Crisis Diplomacy.* Ottawa: Carleton University Press, 1993.

Pearson, Lester. *Words and Occasions.* Toronto: University of Toronto Press, 1970.

_____. *Mike: The Memoirs of the Right Honourable Lester B. Pearson Volume I (1897-1948), II (1948-1957), and III (1957-1968).* Toronto: University of Toronto Press, 1972, 1973, and 1975.

_____. "The Four Faces of Peace," The Honourable Lester Bowles Pearson's Acceptance Speech Upon Presentation of the Nobel Peace Prize in 1957. Uploaded on the Internet with permission from Geoffrey Pearson, son of Lester B. Pearson. www.unac.org/canada/pearson/FAOandUN-Speech_Nobel.html

Credits

The publishers wish to express their gratitude to the following who have given permission to use copyrighted illustrations in this book:
Canada Archives, pages 4(C-018857), 5(C-114756), 7(PA-117622), 12(PA-119892), 13(C-068799), 14(PA-117595), 16(C-007731), 18(C-090374), 19(PA-119013), 20(C-024963), 22(C-014168), 26(PA-117587), 27(PA-123990), 28(PA-117607), 31(C-020020), 32(PA-117617), 34(PA-122737), 35(C-094168), 39(PA-112695), 42(PA-129349), 45(C-015160), 46(PA-185466), 49(PA-110220), 53(PA-142624), 56(PA-093533), 57(PA-117531), 59(PA-121710), 63(C-010435)
Canadian Museum of Contemporary Photography (Ted Grant, NFB Collection), page 52(64-3988)
Every effort has been made to credit all sources correctly. The publishers will welcome any information that will allow them to correct any errors or omissions.

Index

Avro Arrow, 42
Bennett, R.B., 15-16, 17
Borden, Robert, 9, 10
Britain, 3-4, 6-7, 13, 23, 32-33, 48, 55
budget issue, 49-50
Canada Assistance Plan, 52
Canada, international role of, 23, 24-25, 61
Canada Pension Plan, 51
civil service, 14, 15-16
Cold War, 29-30, 31
Commonwealth, 9, 33, 57
Confederation, 4
constitution, 55

death penalty, 54-55
Depression, 16
Diefenbaker, John, 38-39, 40, 42-46
diplomacy, 15, 24, 56
disarmament, 16-17
economy, 16, 42-43
election campaigns, 40, 43, 46, 54
Expo '67, 57-58
external affairs, department of, 13-14
federalism, 43-44, 50-51
flag issue, 52-53
foreign policy, 13, 25, 61
functionalism, 24-25, 26
de Gaulle, Charles, 58
Gordon, Walter, 47, 48, 49-50, 54
Hitler, Adolf, 17, 19, 20
Howe, C.D., 37-38
Imperial War Conference, 9
King, William Lyon Mackenzie, 12-13, 16, 27, 28
Korean War, 31-32
LaMarsh, Judy, 46, 48, 55
Laurier, Wilfrid, 4
leadership style, 39-40, 41, 43, 53, 58, 60-61
League of Nations, 10, 16, 17-18
Lesage, Jean, 43-44, 50
Liberal Party, 47-48
Medicare, 52
minority government, 43, 46, 54
NATO, 30-31
Nobel Peace Prize, 35
NORAD, 44-45
nuclear weapons, 44-45
Paris Peace Conference, 10
peacekeeping force, 33-35
Pearson, Lester
    childhood, 3-5
    and civil service, 15-16, 18, 21-22
    death, 59
    education, 6, 9-10, 11-12
    legacy, 60-61
    marriage, 12
    nervous breakdown, 8
    parents, 4-5
    and politics, 28, 39-40, 41, 58-59
    retirement, 58-59
    and United Nations, 26-27, 29-30
    on WWII, 19-20
Pearson, Maryon (Moody), 12, 41, 55
pipeline, trans-Canada, 37-38
Quebec, 42, 43-44, 50-51, 57-58
"sixty days" promise, 46, 47, 48
Skelton, Dr. O.D., 13, 14, 21
Soviet Union, 29, 32
St. Laurent, Louis, 27-28, 39
Suez Crisis, 32-35
Trudeau, Pierre, 54, 55, 59
United Nations, 25-26, 29-37
United States, 22-24, 45, 55-56
Vietnam War, 56-57
women, status of, 4, 48, 55
World War I, 6-8, 9
World War II, 20, 21, 22-23, 27

THE
NEWJOURNEY
TO WHOLENESS & HOLINESS
PASTOR ROBERT F. LOGGINS, SR.

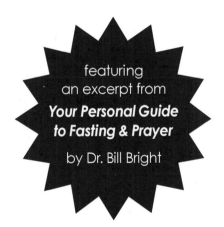

featuring
an excerpt from
*Your Personal Guide
to Fasting & Prayer*

by Dr. Bill Bright

THE
NEWJOURNEY

WRITE YOUR NAME: _____

BEGINNING: DAY OF THE WEEK/MONTH/DATE/YEAR:

_____

40 DAYS

ENDING: DAY OF THE WEEK/MONTH/DATE/YEAR:

_____

FOCUS: GOD
- FATHER
- SON
- HOLY SPIRIT

COMPLETE the following pages. On page 12, respond to this question. **"Why are you on The New Journey?"** Then once you have read **DAY 1**, answer this question. **"What did God say to you today?**

WELCOME TO YOUR THE NEW JOURNEY.

THE NEW JOURNEY TO WHOLENESS & HOLINESS
FASTING AND PRAYING

Robert F. Loggins, Sr., Ministries, LLC
P. O. Box 4261
Chesterfield, MO 63006-4261

Editing: Drena and Melody
Cover and Layout: Randall Nowell

Printed in the United States of America
ISBN: 978-0-9830453-5-9   ISBN: 9-780983-045359

Unless otherwise indicated, all Scripture quotations are taken from the King James Version of the Holy Bible or are the author's revision of that version.

Verses marked NIV are taken from the Holy Bible, the New International Version, copyright© 1973, 1978, 1984 by the International Bible Society. Used by permission of Zondervan. All rights reserved.

Verses marked NLT are taken from the Holy Bible, the New Living Translation, copyright© 1996. Used by permission of Tyndale House Publishers, Inc., Wheaton, IL 60189 USA. All rights reserved.

Verses marked TNIV are taken from the Holy Bible, the Today's New International Version, copyright© 2001, 2005 by International Bible Society.

Verses marked are taken from The Message, copyright© 1993, 1994, 1995, 1996, 2000, 2001, 2002 by Eugene H. Peterson.

Verses marked HCSB are taken from the Holman Christian Standard Bible®, copyright© 1999, 2000, 2002, 2003 by Holman Bible Publishers. Used by permission of Holman Christian Standard Bible®, Holman CSB®, & HCSB® are federally registered trademarks of Holman Bible Publishers.

Verses marked ASV are taken from the American Standard Version online in the public domain.

Verses marked NASV are taken from the New American Standard Version, copyright© 2003, 2002, 2000, 1999 by Lockman Foundation, LaHabra, California

Verses marked NLV are taken from the New Living Version, copyright© 1969 by Christian Literature International.

Dedicated to
Cassandra
My Suitable Helper
(Genesis 2:18)

TABLE OF

Cassandra's New Journey 9

A Welcome From *The New Journey* Team 10

FOREWORD Dr. Gregory R. Frizzell..................................11

Day 1 – The Journey Adventurers......................................13

Day 2 – You Are Not Alone..25

Day 3 – I Seek Thee...29

Day 4 – In The Pit...33

Day 5 – His Throne 37

Day 6 – Sodom, Get Out!..41

Day 7 – Strengthened Hands...45

Day 8 – Justice Prevails...49

Day 9 – If...53

Day 10 – He's Able..57

Day 11 – The Prayer Of Jesus 61

Day 12 – The Prayer Of Jesus Continues..........................65

Day 13 – The Prayer Of Jesus Climax 69

Day 14 – Prayer At Midnight 73

Day 15 – Earnest Prayer..77

Day 16 – In The Fish Belly...81

Day 17 – Look Like Christ 85

Day 18 – Maturing On The Journey...................................89

Day 19 – Be Real 93

Day 20 – Be Angry; Sin Not..97

Day 21 – Be Honest 101

Day 22 – Mouth Cleaning 105

Day 23 – The Heart Matters...109

Day 24 – Live Agape..113

Day 25 – House Cleaning Time...117

CONTENTS

Day 26 – A Life Change 121

Day 27 – Lord, Help!!! 125

Day 28 – Live Wisely 129

Day 29 – Moving From...To 133

Day 30 – The Language Of Love and Peace 137

Day 31 – Biblical Submission 141

Day 32 – The Submitting Wife 145

Day 33 – The Submitting Husband 149

Day 34 – Submitting Children 153

Day 35 – Submitting Fathers 157

Day 36 – Submitting Workers 161

Day 37 – God's Dress Code 165

Day 38 – God's Spirit 169

Day 39 – Deep, Deep Love 173

Day 40 – Godly Determination 177

Peaks And Valleys 181

Appendix I: Small Group Study 185

Appendix II: Guide To Fasting And Prayer 203

Appendix III: Prayer Life 225

Appendix IV: Be Holy 234

Appendix V: Scriptures and Strongholds 239

Appendix VI: Tools For The Journey 245

Appendix VII: Continuing The Journey (CTJ) 256

Prayer List 259

About the Author 261

Join the Journey 262

Prayer Discipleship™ Notes 264

Cassandra's New Journey

I have come to realize that one's life journey is not linear. Rather, life's journey is arranged in a circular fashion. Circularity best describes one's life journey because it is associated with the reality of the human experiences of skirting away, hedging in, revolving around and, most of all, starting over.

The New Journey is my husband's ongoing effort to help each of us in starting over on a new journey to wholeness and holiness. This book, as previously presented in the first Journey, truly is the culmination of my husband's life experiences, passions, and convictions. Pastor Loggins, my husband, loves to help fellow travelers continue on the path of a closer intimacy with the Lord Jesus Christ, a deeper fullness in living wholly and holy unto the Father, and a renewed sense of purpose in applying the Life Principles embedded within the heart and soul of *The New Journey*.

I know this because I have seen these principles transform the lives of people throughout our years of ministry and most recently in Robert's ministry as a North American Missionary and the Prayer and Spiritual Awakening Specialist with our state convention. Many men and women have approached me with stories about how their marriages have been made better, how their job performance increased, and how their families have been made whole. Through these life stories, trials and testimonies, my husband has been able to glean some key insights - life lessons - just for you.

So, do you desire true intimacy with God? If you do then I can testify through personal experience that this new PrayerDiscipleship™ book can present you with the keys to unlock explosive blessings in your life. I beseech you to come with us. Choose now to set out on a New Journey of your own toward a fuller, more intimate relationship with our Heavenly Father. I assure you it will be an adventure that you will never forget nor regret.

– Cassandra Loggins

WELCOME from the Team

Welcome to a new adventure in Christ Jesus - *The New Journey* - PrayerDISCIPLESHIP™ Devotional Journal. You are about to embark on a voyage navigating through the real-life encounters of people who have met God through trials, tribulations and tests. *The New Journey* is designed to encourage you through your struggles and strengthen you in your spiritual walk. This will all come from a steady stream of **Life Stories, Life Principles** and **Life Journeys.** Each day is meant to progressively build you to a point where you too can effectively and powerfully share your testimony. There will be no meaningful testimony without a testing process. Are you up for a test? Your New Journey is ready to begin. Your breakthrough is near.

The success of Pastor Loggins' first *Journey* book, *The Journey to Holiness and Wholeness,* has not been reflected in how many copies that have been distributed, but in how many lives have been touched and transformed. While the out pouring of positive feedback has been tremendous, there is an underlying thirst from the fellowship of believers—that's you—for more. More life, more love, more holiness! *The New Journey* is an answer to this desire for more.

This book is not about imperfect people trying to live perfect lives. Rather, it is simply about ordinary people demonstrating tremendous faith in a wonderful God. This book is about you! I challenge you to find yourself on *The New Journey.* Day one starts now!

The New Journey Team PRAYERDISCIPLES™
R. F. Loggins, Sr., Ministries, LLC

FOREWARD from Dr. Frizzell

When God's Spirit is truly guiding someone's life, it is a wonderful thing to behold. There is no question that the hand of God is guiding the ministry and resources of my friend, Robert Loggins. It is a special joy to commend this new book to the Christian world. As with his other books, *The New Journey* to *Wholeness & Holiness* is filled with Scripture and real life stories. The selected Scriptures and stories deeply touch the heart. On each page readers are brought face to face with God.

In a way that is convicting yet filled with grace, readers see truths that truly transform. Perhaps best of all, *The New Journey* helps believers apply what God is saying to their hearts. All true discipleship involves God-given revelation and experiential application. In a way only God can do, this tool definitely does both! The subjects covered are also amazingly complete. The book touches virtually every issue vital to growth and renewal.

As with all of Bob's resources, the new tool contains a wealth of practical tools any believer can use with ease. The material on fasting is extremely helpful and thorough. The concluding material on strongholds is a perfect way to lead believers into lasting victory. I heartily commend *The New Journey* for individuals, small groups and whole churches. This is truly a journey to revival and growth!

Toward the Next Great Awakening,

Dr. Gregory R. Frizzell
Pastor, Author and Spiritual Awakening Specialist

Why are you on *The New Journey?*

_____

_____

_____

_____

_____

_____

_____

_____

_____

_____

_____

_____

_____

_____

_____

COMPLETE

FOCUS: GOD

Time: _____

Date: _____

Daily Goal:

_____

_____

_____

_____

_____

_____

_____

_____

_____

DAY 1

New Journey Adventurers

"All great adventures begin and end at the throne of grace."

– A wise saying taken from the heart and soul of Hebrews 4:16

THE 40 DAY NEW JOURNEY

This is a work of God and it is my deep desire that the Holy Spirit will truly set you free from the bondage of life's struggles and hindrances. In John 5:1-16 a man needs healing. The Bible does not give us the man's name because he represents all of humanity. Jesus inquired of the crippled man, "Wilt thou be made whole?"

"After this there was a feast of the Jews; and Jesus went up to Jerusalem. Now there is at Jerusalem by the sheep market a pool, which is called in the Hebrew tongue Bethesda, having five porches. In these lay a great multitude of impotent folk, of blind, halt, withered, waiting for the moving of the water. For an angel went down at a certain season into the pool, and troubled the water: whosoever then first after the troubling of the water stepped in was made whole of whatsoever disease he had. And a certain man was there, which had an infirmity thirty and eight years. When Jesus saw him lie, and knew that he had been now a long time in that case, he saith unto him, Wilt thou be made whole? The impotent man answered him, Sir, I have no man, when the water is troubled, to put me into the pool: but while I am coming, another steppeth down before me. Jesus saith unto him, Rise, take up thy bed, and walk. And immediately the man was made whole, and took up his bed, and walked: and on the same day was the sabbath. The Jews therefore said unto him that was cured, It is the sabbath day: it is not lawful for thee to carry thy bed. He answered them, He that made me whole, the same said unto me, Take up thy bed, and walk. Then asked they him, What man is that which said unto thee, Take up thy bed, and walk? And he that

was healed wist not who it was: for Jesus had conveyed himself away, a multitude being in that place. Afterward Jesus findeth him in the temple, and said unto him, Behold, thou art made whole: sin no more, lest a worse thing come unto thee. The man departed, and told the Jews that it was Jesus, which had made him whole. And therefore did the Jews persecute Jesus, and sought to slay him, because he had done these things on the sabbath day." (John 5: 1-16)

I do not know how long you have been crippled in your spiritual walk with God, nor am I aware of your current relationship with the Lord of the Sabbath; nonetheless, in spite of your present standing with Christ, the Lord of the Sabbath, He wants you to take it to the next level. God desires a change in your life. He wants you to stop living a life devoid of devoted conviction and spiritual growth. To succeed, though, you must stop hanging around people who seek to hold you hostage to your painful past, hindering you from finding a peace with God which passes all understanding (Philippians 4:7).

It is time for you to embrace the heart of the Lord of the Sabbath and be made whole. Step out of your crippled condition and walk away from other folks who are holding you down from being completely healed. God wants you to take up your bed and walk!

The New Journey To Wholeness & Holiness will help you achieve the next step. Remember, it is only a step with the aid of the Lord of the Sabbath. He is with you, always! We possess a life-changing power endowed to us by a loving God. To plug into that Heavenly energy source, we must understand that prayer and disciplined fasting will be crucial if we are to achieve true, lasting wholeness and holiness.

LIFE ON THE NEW JOURNEY

Every life story shared in *The New Journey* emerges out of my 40 years of personal ministry and missions at the local, national, and international levels. Every life story in *The New Journey* is real. However, many of the testimonies are changed to prayerfully respect the identity of each person represented in the PrayerDISCIPLESHIP™ Journal. On the other hand, I chose to elevate my mother's (Gladys Louise Loggins) story and those of a few others to bestow honor upon them as great and gifted disciple makers. I wanted this book to be more than "just another devotional journal." *The New Journey* is a first of its kind. That's why, I have identified it as a PrayerDISCIPLESHIP™ Devotional Journal.

What do I mean by PrayerDISCIPLESHIP™? The LORD placed on my heart that we as journey travelers need the "dynamic duo" of prayer (i.e., Holy Spirit Conversation) and the Word (i.e., Jesus Christ the Incarnate Word) to talk with God. PrayerDISCIPLESHIP™ does just that. It blends the most powerful interactive prayer with the mightiest guidance of God's Word to dramatically deepen our intimacy with Christ, God's Only Begotten Son (John 3:16).

As you read the **Life Stories**, allow God to help you see what others have experienced so that you might glean from their encounter – an experience with God. Then, when you read the **Life Principles**, ask the Holy Spirit of God to disciple you. You should desire to grow up and mature (Ephesians 4:14-16); you shouldn't want to remain infantile in your spiritual development. Finally, when you engage in the **Life Journeys**, take time to reflect and allow God to mold you into a more perfect vessel for the Lord's use (Matthew 5-7, the Beatitudes). It is time for each of us to grow up and mature in the new discipline of applying the PrayerDISCIPLESHIP™ Devotional Journal in our daily walk.

Like the original *Journey To Wholeness & Holiness*, *The New Journey To Wholeness & Holiness* begins with a personal introduction to the lame man at the Pool of Bethesda. John 15:1-16 is the heart and soul of *The New Journey*. Allow the Holy Spirit of God to teach you how to minister to spiritually lame and broken people like Jesus ministered to the lame man at the pool. Then pray that God will grant you the same measure of grace to experience personal healing deep within your soul as well. This section is designed for you, as an adventurer, to take your time and allow the Spirit of God to do a deep work in your soul. Please take your time. Allow the Lord time to speak to your heart.

The next major foundational section, which is totally new in *The New Journey*, is "Your Personal Guide to Fasting and Prayer" provided by the gracious permission of Bright Media Foundation. I want to personally thank Brother Tom Doster, the staff and executive board of Bright Media Foundation for allowing me to share what the Holy Spirit of God birthed in Dr. Bright many years ago.

When I discovered what Dr. Bright had done in the area of fasting and prayer, my heart was greatly encouraged. God spoke to me in a clear and concise manner. God said, "You have got to have all of this in *The New Journey*." After numerous emails, prayers, conversations and hours of seeking the heart and face of God, the Lord answered my prayer. At 7:30 a.m. on August 17, 2011, Bright Media Foundation emailed me and granted R. F. Loggins, Sr., Ministries, LLC the right to use Dr. Bright's personal guide to fasting and prayer. Immediately I begin to pray, shout and sing praises to the Lord for His faithfulness and love for my ministry. God had answered my prayer!

You will be greatly blessed by this new addition to *The New Journey To Wholeness & Holiness: Fasting and Praying* 40-Day Devotional Journal. Thank you again Bright Media Foundation for your enormous kindness and compassion to my ministry for God's glory.

Make sure you read every last word of this section. As you read you will learn things such as:

- Why you should fast
- How to fast safely
- How long and what type of fast is right for you
- How to prepare yourself spiritually and physically
- How to manage your schedule while fasting
- How to deal with the responses of friends and loved ones
- How to make your spiritual experience the best it can be
- How to maintain nutritional balance and health from beginning to end (including specific juice & broth recipes)
- What physical benefits to expect
- How to finish your fast and return to your normal schedule in a HEALTHY way

Dr. Bright's insightful biblical passion for seeking the heart and face of God will change your life and your eating habits. You will never be the same (in a good way) as you pray and fast for God's direction in your life.

As you release yourself into the hands of Almighty God, you will be able to complete each exercise in *The New Journey* in 30 minutes or less. However, if you sense God telling you to spend more time with Him, then slow down and allow God to take complete control that day. Take your time. Enjoy each and every day.

The 40 Days of Fasting and Prayer is about applying two very simple, yet powerful, spiritual disciplines. The first discipline is that of prayer. Prayer is simply talking or engaging in a conversation with God. The second discipline is that of fasting. Fasting is a spiritual discipline of abstaining from eating food and engaging in other earthly distractions for a divine purpose or goal.

To help you achieve all God has in store for you, let me give you the five easy steps for every traveler on *The New Journey*:

STEP 1: Read and meditate on the Scripture passage

STEP 2: Read the Life Story Message

STEP 3: Read the Life Principle Application

STEP 4: In the Life Journey Experience, write your own personal life reflection

STEP 5: *The New Journey* Prayer

Pray, following the acrostic **A.C.T.S.** (**Adoration**, **Confession**, **Thanksgiving** and **Supplication**), and begin your fast. *The New Journey* fast consists of fasting from food, viewing television, listening to secular radio, music, DVD's, CD's, movies, emails and/or internet surfing while practicing periods of absolute silence.

The following is an explanation of each letter in the **A.C.T.S.** acrostic:

A is for Adoration. Adoration is defined as "an expression of great love, devotion and respect to someone or something. In the context of Christian prayer, adoration occurs when one engages in worshiping or paying homage to God."[1]

C is for Confession. Confession is "the act of acknowledging sin or admitting guilt for an infraction one has committed in the offense of another."[2] When it comes to Christian confession, 1 John 1:9 is often referred to: "*If we confess our sins, he is faithful and just to forgive us our sins, and to cleanse us from all unrighteousness.*" Prayer without confession of sin is like apologizing for a wrongful act against one's brother or sister without being deeply sorry.

T is for Thanksgiving. Thanksgiving is defined as "an expression of gratitude, often public in giving thanks to God in the form of a prayer."[3] 1 Thessalonians 5:18 (NIV) says, "*give thanks in all circumstances...*" Thanksgiving is directly connected to our Christian attitude (Philippians 2:5).

---

[1] Michael Agnes, Editor in Chief, *Webster's New World College Dictionary Fourth Edition*, "Adoration" (New York: Macmillan USA, 1999), 19.
[2] Ibid, "Confession," 305.
[3] Ibid, "Thanksgiving," 1482.

S is for Supplication. Supplication implies "standing in the gap." In Ezekiel 22:30 God said, "*I looked for a man who would build up the wall and stand in the gap on behalf of the land so I wouldn't have to destroy it, but I found none.*"

An example of standing in the gap is when we pray for others. As Christians, we are not only to pray to God for our own pressing concerns, but we are to equally pray for others as well. Supplication is a form of intercessory prayer. God has called us as Christians to engage in the ministry of intercessory prayer. In *The New Journey*, you will be afforded the opportunity to create your own intercessory prayer list. Prayer and fasting is the heart and soul of *The New Journey*.

Now let me provide an example of an **A.C.T.S. Prayer:**

- **Adoration** - "Lord, we adore Thee. You are an awesome God.

- **Confession** - " Lord I have sinned and fallen short of Your glory. Please forgive me, Lord. I am sorry."

- **Thanksgiving** - "Dear Lord, I just want to thank You for all that You have done for me. You have been so good to me and I know I don't deserve all of your goodness."

- **Supplication** - "Dear Lord, I am standing in the gap for my kids, my spouse, my boss, my friends, my church and family, etc."

Remember that Prayer in the Spirit is not a human template such as the **Model Prayer** and **A.C.T.S. Prayer** in the Spirit only occurs when the heart of man moves the heart of God. Therefore, learn to use both the **Model Prayer** and **A.C.T.S.** to assist you in coming into the presence of God to achieve Prayer in the Spirit.

The New Journey is work. Fasting and praying are some of the most difficult tasks in which Christians can engage on a daily basis. However, there are great benefits and blessings to be reaped through the spiritual discipline of having a personal devotional life with God.

The next section in *The New Journey* is the conclusion. I call this section "Peaks and Valleys." Why? In this section I encourage you to share the peaks, for they are profound and joyous. On the other hand, I also encourage you to share your valleys. Peaks and valleys are normal human realities. Learn the value of maximizing your peaks and managing your valleys. In the peaks and valleys section, you will discover how joy can be found in life's valley as well as on the mountain top. Peaks and valleys are essentially life's highs and lows. What I want you to learn as you travel your new Christian journey is how to maintain balance despite how deep you fall or how high you climb. It is my prayer that you will learn how to equally embrace life's highs and lows. God uses peaks and valleys to teach us, to grow us and to mature us as His people.

Following the section on peaks and valleys, you will be encouraged to utilize *The New Journey's* seven appendixes. **Appendix I** is the "Small Group New Journey Eight-Week Study." Under the leadership of your pastor and church leaders, start a small group in your church, on your job or in your community. The goal is to guide people to the deepest purpose and meaning of prayer.

Appendix II is a "Guide to Fasting and Prayer: Seven Basic Steps to Successful Fasting and Prayer" by Dr. Bill Bright and Campus Crusade for Christ International. You will be equipped to understand the practical and biblical importance of fasting and praying.

Appendix III is "Prayer Life," which focuses on the teachings of Jesus in "The Model Prayer." Jesus sets the template for an effective and successful prayer life as He instructs His disciples in how to pray. You will also be challenged to apply the "Food Guidelines" throughout your travel on *The New Journey*. This may be a new discipline for many of you, but if you will trust God and follow the guidelines, you will be blessed and strengthened.

Appendix IV is entitled "Be Holy." Wholeness is always preceded by holiness. Holiness is learning to live in a right relationship with God and man. There will never be complete wholeness until there is genuine holiness.

Appendix V on "Scriptures and Strongholds" employs the power of God's Word as He smashes ungodliness while knocking down the various strongholds that try to hinder His Kingdom work on Earth.

Appendix VI, entitled "Tools for the Journey," provides biblical tools to enable the journey traveler to uproot deep anger, crippling anxieties, an unforgiving heart and inappropriate use of words and language.

Appendix VII, which is identified as "CTJ – Continuing the Journey," empowers the journey traveler to press on toward revival and spiritual awakening. Revival is for the church body while spiritual awakening is for the larger lost community. When we as Christians authentically live the Christian life, lost men and women can hear God's calling on their own lives and allow themselves to be drawn to Him as they observe our humble obedience to our Master and our faithful service to our Maker.

As we obey and serve God, remember this: people need prayer. It is prayer which not only goes beyond words, but shakes the very throne room of God. So, prayerfully use your "Prayer Disciples Prayer List" to practice praying for lost souls and loved ones to come to experience the joy of being made whole and holy through Christ (John 5).

The New Journey To Wholeness & Holiness: Guide to Fasting & Prayer is about being made whole and holy, both physically and spiritually. Once you step on the path of your new journey, don't waver, stop or detour. Finish your adventure as you climb to the summit, reach your ultimate destination and celebrate with Christ.

When this occurs you will be able to do what I learned to do when I was in the sixth grade. I was chosen by my sixth grade performing arts teacher to be in our annual musical production. She came to me and said, "Robert, you have been chosen to be in the annual sixth grade musical this year." I was flabbergasted. Fear gripped me and I froze stiff like an arctic glacier. I experienced a mental block in learning my 17 lines in the musical as one of the key performers. However, when I stopped to really listen to the words of our theme song, my fear evaporated into thin air and I performed with poise, precision and perfection (if I do say so myself). The song was "Climb Every Mountain"[4] from *The Sound of Music*:

Climb Ev'ry Mountain,
Ford Evr'y stream,
Follow Evr'y rainbow,
'Till you find your dream.
A dream that will need
All the love you can give,
Ev'ry day of your life
For as long as you live.
Climb ev'ry mountain,
Ford ev'ry stream,
Follow every rainbow,
Till you find your dream
A dream that will need
All the love you can give,
Ev'ry day of your life,
For as long as you live.
Climb ev'ry mountain,
Ford ev'ry stream,
Follow evr'y rainbow,
Till You Find Your Dream.

[4]The Sound of Music, "Climb Every Mountain," http://www.lyrics007 .com/Sound%20 Of%20Music%20Lyrics/Climb%20Every%20Mountain%20Lyrics.html.

Allow the lyrics of this song to empower you to relentlessly complete *The New Journey*. As you begin, you are one step closer toward achieving your goal. Every journey begins with a single step. That first step, often the most terrifying, is followed by one more and another after that. Each step you take carries you closer to the goal for which you strive. No excursion has ever been completed, no mountain summit ever reached, without that first step. One last encouragement as you gird yourself for that first step: in your climb to your own summit, whether you find yourself on a soaring peak or a dark valley, I urge you to pause along the way and admire the view!

Keep Climbing,
Pastor Robert F. Loggins

Personal Life Reflection: What did God say to you today?

_____

_____

_____

_____

_____

_____

_____

_____

_____

_____

DAY 2

FOCUS: GOD

Time: _____

Date: _____

Daily Goal:

_____

_____

_____

_____

_____

_____

_____

_____

_____

You Are Not Alone

"He who has a *why* to live can bear with almost any *how*."

– Nietzsche, from Vicktor E. Frankl, *Man's Search for Meaning*, p. 9

LIFE STORY

You Are Not Alone
Read and Meditate: 1 Kings 18:16-24

"And call ye on the name of your gods, and I will call on the name of the LORD: and the God that answereth by fire, let him be God" (1 Kings 18:24a).

Freddy was so frightened he was unable to move. At nine years old he was living out his greatest fear of being left at home alone. Now his worst nightmare had come true and he was paralyzed with fear.

Faith and fear are from two different seeds. Fear is from the seed of Adam (Genesis 3) whereas faith is from the seed of Abraham (Hebrews 11). Faith in the Lord always trumps fear. Elijah was a man of faith. Outnumbered by the priests who ate at Jezebel's table, Elijah was not afraid. Faith in God always arrives in the nick of time for those who are willing to face insurmountable challenges. You will never experience the comfort in knowing what you can overcome if you have never been consumed by the fire of faith. God is greater than the odds against you.

Unfortunately, far too many Christians will never discover a faith that is greater than their fear unless, and until, they refuse to stop leaning on the human crutch of fear. God is able to remove our fear, but if He does, it actually thwarts our faith development. You will never learn the secret of facing your fear with faith if your fear fails to challenge your faith. Giant faith can't be taught in a Bible study – it must be experienced. You will remain oblivious of Abrahamic faith in God as long as you remain with one toe on the ground of comfort and the other toe on self-proclaimed courage of "gab." Faith is action and action is visibly revealed by fire! You are never home alone.

LIFE PRINCIPLE

Today's Life Principle: *Understanding.* How do we apply this Life Principle on Day 2? What must we understand about our fear before we can overcome it? We need to understand the **"Seven Critical Truths That Cancel Every Traveler's Fear"**:

1. Fear fractures our faith in God.
2. Fear troubles our heart, health, wholeness, holiness and peace with God.
3. Fear competes with our faith in God.
4. Fear must be confronted through a public display of our confidence in God's power.
5. God uses victory over fear to build our fellowship, foundation, faith and future success for His glory.
6. The size and magnitude of our enemy (i.e., fear) is no match for the size and magnitude of our God (i.e., faith) who answers by fire.
7. The battle to defeat our faith with fear is a never-ending struggle.

You must understand and live by convictions based on God's holy, righteous and life-sustaining Word. You are not (i.e., never) alone when God is within you (2 Corinthians 5:17). If God is for you, no one can stand against you and succeed. Be on guard because the evil spirits of Ahab and Jezebel are always lurking in the shadows of a mind lacking faith in God. Remember, achieving God's best begins with faith and confidence in the God who answers by fire. Never eat at Jezebel's table. Face your foes with faith. Never allow the odds against you to be greater than the One within you – Christ (Colossians 1:15-20). Completely trust God (Proverbs 3:5-6).

LIFE JOURNEY

Personal Life Reflection: What did God say to you today?

_____

_____

_____

_____

_____

_____

The New Journey Prayer using A.C.T.S. (Adoration, Confession, Thanksgiving and Supplication – page 19-20):

1. Ask the Lord to give you an unfathomable understanding that you are never alone as a traveler on your new journey.

2. Pray that God will help you apply the principles of fasting and praying throughout the entire journey adventure.

3. Prayerfully read Appendix II, "Guide to Fasting and Prayer," pages 203-224. Pray that the Holy Spirit will empower you to seek God's wisdom in following the guide out of a spirit of humble obedience instead of a spirit of obligatory legalism.

4. Begin your daily prayer list and add to it as the Holy Spirit of God guides you. Refer to the "Prayer Disciples Prayer List" on pages 259-260.

Fast: Abstain from eating one meal.

DAY 3

FOCUS: GOD

Time: _____

Date: _____

Daily Goal:

_____

_____

_____

_____

_____

_____

_____

_____

_____

I Seek Thee

"The pouring out of His soul is the divine meaning of intercession."

– Andrew Murray & C. H. Spurgeon, *The Believer's Secret of Intercession*, (Compiler, L. G. Parkhurst, Jr.), p. 45

LIFE STORY

I Seek Thee in the Morning
Read and Meditate: Psalm 5:3-12

"My voice shalt thou hear in the morning, O Lord; in the morning will I direct my prayer unto thee, and will look up" (Psalm 5:3).

Victor was hooked for life. He called it "keeping the morning watch" and it had become his passion. Before the break of day he was down on his knees listening and communing with the LORD. King David understood the passion of all the Victors in the family of God. Rising and peeling out of his toasty, warm bed was not always a pleasured celebration. Often it is a gruesome and bemoaning task for Vic. We should at all cost, keep the morning watch.

Something happens in the fresh dew drop hours of the early morning. The air is pure and still. You can literally hear your heart thumping as it pumps fresh streams of blood throughout your entire body. I have come to learn that in the early morning God's voice is the most impactful. Like thunder His voice rumbles and echoes throughout the chambers of my soul. It is in these quiet and still moments of the day when God makes His loudest proclamation deep within me. I have come to discover God's perfect will, not just His permissive will for my life. God's permissive will is God's allowance for Man, but God's perfect will is God's affirmation for Man.

David was confronted with wickedness, foolishness, iniquity, destruction, deceitfulness, ungodly flatter, transgression and rebellion at its worst. Yet, David chose to trust God with great joy (Proverbs 3:5-6). David understood what it meant to have the Lord's favor and divine protection shielding him from the dangers of evil men. David said, *"…in the morning will I direct my prayers unto thee, and will look up"* (Psalm 5:3). Let us habitually seek the Lord in the stillness of the morning with a bold passion and a deep thirst for more and more of God.

LIFE PRINCIPLE

Today's Life Principle: *Understanding.* How do we apply this Life Principle on Day 3? It is accomplished through understanding the fears all *New Journey* travelers must overcome and follow the **"Ten Commandments of a Fearless Traveler"**:

1. Release your fears over to God and embrace the mind of Christ (Philippians 2:5).
2. Open your heart to hear the still, quiet voice of God say, "Fear not."
3. Humble your life over to the will of God as opposed to the will of man's fears.
4. Determine to use your tongue to glorify God and encourage others to fear not.
5. Allow the hands of God to build bridges of understanding over all your fears.
6. Use your feet to rush into knowing how to extinguish all your fears.
7. Use the eyes of your heart to see fearful people delivered by Jesus from all fears.
8. Fill your mouth full of godly wisdom to banish the spirit of fear at all times.
9. Use your tongue to praise and worship God in the midst of your fears (Psalm 150).
10. Surrender all your fears over to the Lord of the harvest to win souls (Matthew 9:38).

Determine to make it a godly priority to seek God's face before you start your day. Without apology thirst for God's heart, mind, will and purpose for your life. Whenever there are roadblocks hindering you from seeking the face of God in the early morning, develop a habit of praying this prayer before you drift off to sleep: "Precious Lord, don't allow anything to come between you and me. But Lord, if it does, immediately remove it. In Jesus' name, Amen."

LIFE JOURNEY

Personal Life Reflection: What did God say to you today?

_____

_____

_____

_____

_____

_____

_____

The New Journey Prayer using A.C.T.S. (Adoration, Confession, Thanksgiving and Supplication – page 19-20):

1. Pray that you will desire to seek the Lord at all times.
2. Determine to make it a personal priority to seek God's face daily.
3. Ask God to unclutter your heart and unshackle your mind so that knowing God's will becomes a habit.

Fast: **Abstain from one meal, listening to secular music, DVD's, CD's and from viewing movies.**

DAY 4

In the Pit

"Weak stomachs prefer bland diets, but strong stomachs never refuse any meat set before them; all fare is alike to them."

– William Gurnall, *The Christian in Complete Armour*, p. 394

LIFE STORY

Life in the Pit
Read and Meditate: Psalm 88:1-18

"O LORD God of my salvation, I have cried day and night before Thee ...Thou hast laid me in the lowest pit, in darkness, in the deeps" (Ps. 88:1).

When the baby died, a part of Mary died as well. Mary wept bitterly every day for nine months. Mary found herself imprisoned in a pit of shame and disappointment. On the first day of the tenth month, Mary dried her eyes, washed her face, put on some new clothes and went out to dinner with her husband. One can choose either to die in the pit or step up out of the dungeon and live a full and meaningful life in Christ. God often appoints His choice servants to "The Pit." The Pit is not necessarily used for punishment; rather God employs these pits for spiritual refinement.

In this scripture passage, the Psalmist is in a dismal condition. It is the best condition to be in because it holds the potential for a Spirit-Anointed, God-Sent revival. The author of this most insightful Psalm has a recurring theme: one must learn to suffer well. Suffering well suggests that we learn the value of being identified as a believer in the One and Only Begotten Son of God – Jesus Christ. It matters not how you live your life, you will never get to heaven without spending time in the pit. You may only find yourself in the pit for a brief period of time, but rest assured, God will deliver you in due season from your pit just like He delivered Mary from her pit.

The Psalmist had learned numerous lessons. He learned about the pit of affliction, suffering and distraction. His eyes were gushing with tears. His hope was crushed. His peace had been stolen. His strength had wasted away. He was in the pit. Life without a pit is life absent of spiritual growth.

LIFE PRINCIPLE ✕

Today's Life Principle: *Growth.* How do we apply this Life Principle on Day 4? By realizing the **"15 Progressive Stages of Spiritual Growth"** as we emerge from a pit:

Stage 1   – **Utter *Shock***: "Why me, Lord?"

Stage 2   – **Blatant *Denial***: "What did I do wrong?"

Stage 3   – **Profound *Pain***: "Lord, I am dying."

Stage 4   – **Personal *Guilt***: "I must have some unrepentant sin buried beneath the surface of my soul."

Stage 5   – **Boiling *Anger***: "Lord, I'm so angry at you."

Stage 6   – **Frantic *Bargaining***: "Lord, let's make a deal."

Stage 7   – **Deep *Depression***: "I'm going to die down here in this God-forsaken, bottomless pit."

Stage 8   – **Nagging *Reflection***: "If I would have only listened to God."

Stage 9   – **Arctic *Loneliness***: "I feel so alone. Is there anyone on earth who really cares for me?"

Stage 10 – **Looking *Upward***: "I may be in my personal pit, but I refuse to give up."

Stage 11 – **The *U-Turn***: "Lord, it's time for a change in my attitude."

Stage 12 – ***Refocusing***: "Lord Jesus, I can see more clearly now."

Stage 13 – **Laboring through *Disappointments***: "I admit that I am disappointed, but I won't quit."

Stage 14 – **Believing *God***: "My God can do anything but fail" (Psalm 23, 27, 121; Isaiah 40:31; John 15:1-9; Ephesians 3:20-21; Romans 8:28; Philippians 4:13).

Stage 15 – **Embracing Biblical *Faith*, *Hope* and *Love***: "Lord, thank you for loving me while I was shackled in my sins in the pit of death, hell and destruction. Thank You that today, Lord, I'm free" (John 8).

LIFE JOURNEY

Personal Life Reflection: What did God say to you today?

_____

_____

_____

_____

_____

_____

_____

The New Journey Prayer using A.C.T.S. (Adoration, Confession, Thanksgiving and Supplication – page 19-20):

1. Are you in a pit? Do you need to pray?
2. Learn how to pray always. Pray when you are being cast into a pit and pray when you are being lifted up out of a pit. Stop and pray right where you are. Now!
3. Pray for Godly wisdom when you encounter others who are in a pit and they are utterly oblivious to it.
4. Ask God to use your pit for His purpose.

Fast: Abstain from one meal, listening to secular music, DVD's, CD's and from viewing movies.

DAY 5

FOCUS: GOD

Time: _____

Date: _____

Daily Goal:

_____

_____

_____

_____

_____

_____

_____

_____

_____

His Throne

"The Cross is
the pathway to
life in Christ."

– Andrew Murray,
*The Secret of
Spiritual Strength*,
p. 69

LIFE STORY

The Journey to His Throne
Read and Meditate: Hebrews 4:14-16

"Therefore let us approach the throne of grace with boldness, so that we may receive mercy and find grace to help us at the proper time" (Heb. 4:16).

My father was a brutally harsh, ill-reproachable, herculean West Virginia coal miner. He worked hard but lived even harder. I remember seeing my father arriving home in the darkest of night. To this day, I cannot recall ever having breakfast with my father. He worked night and day for almost all of my adolescent years. I needed my father, but my father wasn't there. I wish someone could have told me how to better connect with him.

My Heavenly Father is the total opposite of my earthly father. He's my journey partner and guide. We converse daily. He's patient, compassionate, gentle, loving and kind. Ironically, He has an uncanny way of spending loads of time with all His children. Unlike my earthly father who worked himself to death, my Heavenly Father worked to make us whole and holy by providing us with abundant life. The author of Hebrews says, *"Therefore let us approach the throne of grace with boldness…"* Boldness implies freedom from fear of any repercussions. Our Heavenly Father desires time alone with each and every one of us. Personal time with God the Father carries with it a return on our time investment. Our Father lavishes us with not only grace (i.e., God's unmerited favor) but also His mercy (i.e., God's patience which overrides His punishment). Use these acrostics to help remember two crucial concepts: **GRACE** is God's Riches At Christ's Expense while **MERCY** is the Master's Eternal Restraint Coming despite Your sinful ways. Both Grace and Mercy are found at God's throne.

LIFE PRINCIPLE

Today's **Life Principle:** *By-Products.* How do we apply this Life Principle on Day 5? By learning the **"Ten By-products of One Who Has Spent Time Before the Throne of God's Grace and Mercy"**:

1. Allow God to build *CHARACTER.*
2. Engage in effective and productive *COMMUNICATION* to bring honor and glory to God.
3. Use excellent *LISTENING* skills. Know how to listen with your heart.
4. Value *RELATIONSHIPS* more than resources. People are more valuable than personal gain.
5. Have great *VISION.* Be able to see the future as you dip into the reservoir of God's knowledge and understanding.
6. Employ profound *PASSION.* Be passionately driven to return to God your very best. Believe God desires first fruits. First fruits is an Old Testament manner of communicating that God wants the best of your best before anyone else receives anything.
7. Possess a positive, godly *ATTITUDE* at all times. Be capable of seeing the good in the midst of the bad. Have a keen eye for the unseen and unknown to the human eye.
8. Celebrate *RESPONSIBILITY* as if it were a precious gem. Know irresponsibility is the by-product of the foolish. Responsibility is the by-product of seeking the blessings of the Lord God (Psalm 1).
9. Realize that making wise decisions is the hallmark of *WISDOM.* Be unafraid of earthly failure due to promised Heavenly success.
10. Appreciate the spirit of *HUMILITY* gained from salvation.

LIFE JOURNEY

Personal Life Reflection: What did God say to you today?

_____

_____

_____

_____

_____

_____

_____

The New Journey Prayer using A.C.T.S. (Adoration, Confession, Thanksgiving and Supplication – page 19-20):

1. Thank God for allowing you to have the privilege of entering into His presence with thanksgiving as His child.

2. Praise God for His grace and mercy right now. Close your eyes as tight as possible and do it right where you are.

3. Pray to your Heavenly Father about all the fathers in your church who need to know that they can be saved by the grace of God (Ephesians 2:8-9).

Fast: **Abstain from one meal, listening to secular music, DVD's, CD's and from viewing movies.**

DAY 6

FOCUS: GOD

Time: _____

Date: _____

Daily Goal:

_____

_____

_____

_____

_____

_____

_____

_____

_____

Sodom, Get Out!

"Churches get in ruts only because individuals get in ruts. It is impossible that the church should do anything that individuals do not do."

– A. W. Tozer (Compiler, James L. Snyder), *Rut, Rot or Revival: The Condition of the Church*, p.34

LIFE STORY

Pray for Sodom
Read and Meditate: Genesis 18:16-33

"And the LORD said, Because the cry of Sodom and Gomorrah is great, and because their sin is very grievous; I will go down now, and see whether they have done altogether according to the cry of it, which is come unto me; and if not, I will know. And the men turned their faces from thence, and went toward Sodom: but Abraham stood yet before the LORD" (Gen. 18:20-22).

John Strong refused to stoop to the constant avaricious changes in the volatile insurance business just to make a buck. John was a man of integrity. His perspective of integrity had more to do with motives than with methods. John was a principle-driven, godly business man who was highly respected in the global insurance market.

Like John, Abraham was a man of godly integrity. Unlike the men of Sodom, he was grieved over the outcry that had reached him announcing the great sin of Sodom. What did Abraham do? He simply stood before the Lord pleading his case like a defense attorney, seeking mercy and not justice on behalf of the licentious cities of Sodom and Gomorrah. The mark of a godly man is measured by the stand he takes for righteousness in God's courtroom. Despite the unmitigated evidence against the cities, Abraham persisted in negotiating his case before God for the deliverance of the two wicked cities. Abraham wanted wholeness and holiness to sanctify the sin-sick cities of Sodom and Gomorrah. Like Abraham, we too must plead our case to God for the city of Sodom.

LIFE PRINCIPLE ✖

Today's Life Principle: *The Ministry of Prayer.* How do we apply this Life Principle on Day 6? By sharing the **"Nine Requirements of an Effective Prayer Ministry"** which require:

1. *Sincere Commitment* to the Lord Jesus Christ when praying for the spirit of Sodom to be eradicated.

2. *Personal and/or Corporate Consecration* to purge the stench of Sodom out of the House of God.

3. *Genuine Praise and Worship* that occurs when the remnants of Sodom and Gomorrah are uprooted and exorcised.

4. *A Heart of Exuberant, Contagious Thanksgiving* to the God of Creation when the spirit of Sodom no longer looms as God's people journey daily.

5. *The Work of the Holy Spirit* to serve as a Counselor in squelching the spirit of Sodom.

6. *Agreement with God* in never allowing the spirit of Sodom to invade God's camp and the Lord's people.

7. *Unity in the Body of Christ* to maintain wholeness and holiness in the temple of God.

8. *Daily Intercession* to strengthen the Body of Christ to continue to purge out the spirit of Sodom.

9. *Genuine Discernment* to distinguish the voices of Sodom and Gomorrah from the voice of Almighty God.

LIFE JOURNEY

Personal Life Reflection: What did God say to you today?

_____

_____

_____

_____

_____

_____

_____

The New Journey Prayer using A.C.T.S. (Adoration, Confession, Thanksgiving and Supplication – page 19-20):

1. Ask God to either keep you out of Sodom or lead you out of Sodom.
2. Pray for people you know who are in Sodom. Refer to your prayer list and place their names on your daily prayer list as you cry out to God for them by name (pages 259-260).
3. Determine this day to become an active participant in the prayer ministry of your church or start a New Journey Small Group Eight Week Prayer Study.

Fast: Abstain from eating one meal, opening email for one hour and observe one hour of absolute silence.

DAY 7

FOCUS: GOD

Time: _____

Date: _____

Daily Goal:

_____

_____

_____

_____

_____

_____

_____

_____

_____

Strengthened Hands

"I will greet this day with love in my heart."

– Og Mandino, *The Greatest Salesman in the World*, p. 58

LIFE STORY

The Kind of Prayer that Strengthens Hands
Read and Meditate: Nehemiah 6:5-9

"…Now therefore, O God, strengthen my hands" (Nehemiah 6:9b).

Following numerous failed medical treatments to reduce the lumps around her lungs, Carol decided to return home from M. D. Anderson Cancer Center in Houston, Texas to simply live her life as normal as possible. Carol and John had been happily married for 25 years. This was the year they had planned to travel to all the Hawaiian Islands to celebrate their Silver Anniversary, but her cancer diagnosis shattered their dream vacation plans and hopes for the future.

However, Carol and John did not realize that their tenth-grade boys and girls Sunday School class had decided to pray for them. The kids decided to give up watching TV, video games, movies, fast food and dates for as long as it took for God to heal Carol. God heard their cry. Within one month before John cancelled their dream vacation, Carol appeared to be miraculously improving. A week later John suggested to Carol that they call Dr. Mansfield at Anderson for an appointment. Without hesitation the appointment was scheduled. Carol and John arrived at Anderson and to their utter surprise, after numerous extensive tests and diagnostic evaluations, Carol's cancer had disappeared.

In the same way, prayer removed the threat of Sanballat, Tobiah, and Gershem while strengthening the hands of Nehemiah and the people of God to rebuild the wall. When we decide to genuinely seek the face of God in prayer, the Lord will strengthen our hands and satisfy our hearts.

LIFE PRINCIPLE ⚒

Today's Life Principle: *40 Traits of a Modern Day Nehemiah*. How do we apply this Life Principle on Day 7? Check any or all of the Traits that best identify you:

☐ BRAVE	☐ STEADY	☐ PERSISTENT	☐ UNYIELDING
☐ COURAGEOUS	☐ STEADFAST	☐ CONSTANT	☐ STRONGWILLED
☐ INTREPID	☐ SERIOUS	☐ UNCHALLENGEABLE	☐ TENACIOUS
☐ VALIANT	☐ DECISIVE	☐ FIXED	☐ DOGGED
☐ FIRM	☐ UNSHAKEN	☐ STAUNCH	☐ SELF-RELIANT
☐ DETERMINED	☐ PERSEVERING	☐ STRONG	☐ ENDURING
☐ RESOLVED	☐ PERSISTANT	☐ FAITHFUL	☐ TIRELESS
☐ UNWAVERING	☐ UNFALTERING	☐ UNCOMPROMISING	☐ PURPOSEFUL
☐ SINGLE-MINDED	☐ UNSHAKABLE	☐ IMMOVABLE	☐ UNFLINCHING
☐ ESTABLISHED	☐ INDEPENDENT	☐ DRIVEN	☐ UNREMITTING

In Nehemiah 4:20b, Nehemiah said, "…*our God shall fight for us.*" Impeccable confidence is always rooted in the rich soil of one's unyielding faith. When your faith is unwavering you are able to stand firmly on the holy ground of God Almighty. Nehemiah's "default setting" was fixed on the sovereignty of God, thus he uttered, "*O God, strengthen my hands.*"

LIFE JOURNEY

Personal Life Reflection: What did God say to you today?

_____

_____

_____

_____

_____

_____

_____

_____

The New Journey Prayer using A.C.T.S. (Adoration, Confession, Thanksgiving and Supplication – page 19-20):

1. Confess to God that there are times when you need profound strengthening of your soul and inner peace within your heart.
2. Pray for someone you know who is suffering profusely while going through chemotherapy or some unusual protracted medical treatment.
3. Study the "Model Prayer" on pages 226-231 then examine Richard J. Foster's expression and explanation of the Prayer of Rest on page 228.

Fast: Abstain from eating two meals, viewing television all day and surfing the Internet.

DAY 8

FOCUS: GOD

Time: _____

Date: _____

Daily Goal:

_____

_____

_____

_____

_____

_____

_____

_____

_____

Justice Prevails

"Christians are not to be anxious or worried about anything."

– James Montgomery Boice, *How to Live the Christian Life*, p. 91

LIFE STORY

Justice Will Prevail
Read and Meditate: Habakkuk 1:2-4

"O LORD, how long shall I cry, and thou wilt not hear! Even cry out unto thee of violence, and thou wilt not save!" (Hab. 1:2).

Liberated by the Nuremberg War Crime Trials, a small group of Holocaust survivors traveled back to Europe as a testimony of the prevailing power of human justice over Adolf Hitler's Nazi Germany. Hitler's evil regime had collapsed. The Nazi death camps were now a fading memory. The countless atrocities that they had witnessed as little children were finally over. They had seen mothers, fathers, sisters, brothers, uncles, aunts, doctors, lawyers and countless other innocent people leave on train rides to Auschwitz-Birkenau and never return. This meager group of Holocaust survivors learned what it means to be "liberated in due season." They learned that liberation is more than just returning to a normal life. Liberation means responsibility. It is a humanitarian type of responsibility to remind the civilized world to never load trains to Auschwitz-Birkenau again or doom human lives to the death chambers of evil.

Habakkuk's message to God's chosen people was a message of profound struggle. The question they lived with daily was, "How could God allow the wicked nation of Chaldea to crush His people and still be a loving God?" God's chosen people had to learn that wholeness and holiness is forged out of a furnace of suffering and death. Justice will always prevail. God often employs profuse pain in producing precious people to transform this sinful world and experience abundant life. For Christians, we know death is the doorway to life eternal. This is where ultimate justice prevails.

LIFE PRINCIPLE

Today's Life Principle: *Hope.* How do we apply this Life Principle on Day 8? By discovering in which of the **"Five Levels of Hope"** you are operating today:

1. **Hope Within the Human Soul.** There is a hope that lies within all of us as human beings on Planet Earth.

2. **Hope in Mankind.** This hope gravitates man toward man. It is a hope seeking community and fellowship. Its purpose rests upon discovering where one belongs and the acceptance one can receive from a fellowship community.

3. **Hope in a System of Beliefs.** This hope is driven by philosophical and intellectual patterns of rationalizing one's world view. Human thoughts are at work on numerous levels daily. The challenge is one's focus. Human systems of beliefs interfacing with other human systems of beliefs are often conflicting, compromising, competitive, contaminating and confusing. The underlying and perplexing question is, "Why does God allow such diversity?" Would it not have been much wiser to have simply established two or three systems of belief for all mankind? If so, God would have had to crush the free will of man by imposing His Divine Will over by imposing His Divine Will over Man's human will. God could not allow Himself to engage in such behavior.

4. **Hope in Nature and Creation.** This is hope in Man's best effort on Earth. It is hope in the creation, rather than hope in the Sovereign Creator. This hope demands an eternal quest to be comforted by the Sovereign Creator.

5. **Hope in the God of Creation.** This is the ultimate level of hope, God's premier hope. It is the hope that Habakkuk encountered – life-changing hope. It transforms lives eternally. On which level do you find yourself today?

LIFE JOURNEY

Personal Life Reflection: What did God say to you today?

_____

_____

_____

_____

_____

_____

_____

The New Journey Prayer using A.C.T.S. (Adoration, Confession, Thanksgiving and Supplication – page 19-20):

1. Of "The Five Levels of Hope," which one best describes your level of hope today?
2. How do you operate around wickedness or wicked-spirited people?
3. Repent of the times when you possessed a spirit that dishonored the Lord.
4. Are you keeping your prayer list? Refer to pages 259-260. Place your pastor and his family on your daily prayer list.

Fast: Abstain from eating one meal and practice four hours of absolute silence.

DAY 9

FOCUS: GOD

Time: _____

Date: _____

Daily Goal:

_____

_____

_____

_____

_____

_____

_____

_____

_____

If

"God gives man
time for communion
with Himself."

– Andrew Murray,
An Exciting New Life,
p. 192

 LIFE STORY

If

Read and Meditate: 2 Chronicles 7:14

"If my people, which are called by my name, shall humble themselves, and pray, and seek my face, and turn from their wicked ways; then will I hear from heaven, and will forgive their sin, and will heal their land" (2 Chron. 7:14).

"Dad, during our district soccer match, Joe taunted me to my face in front of my friends and family. He called me a wimp. So I kicked the soccer ball as hard as I could directly at Joe's face. The ball ricocheted off his face and dribbled into the net, scoring the winning goal." Within seconds Sarah shattered both a lifelong friendship and crushed major bones in Joe's face. Following the soccer match, Sarah and Joe never restored their fractured relationship. Sarah's team won the soccer match but she lost the respect of Joe and their lifelong friendship.

What is the price of a fractured relationship? How much does it cost to shatter one's relationship with the Lord? To complete *The New Journey to Wholeness and Holiness* you must learn how to maintain genuine relationships at all cost. Disrespect always results in crushing and shattering once loved and cherished relationships. Well established relationships ought to mean something. They meant something to God, but to His chosen people, their relationship was questionable. God said to them, "If you do these things…then…I will do these things for you." This is known as a conditional statement. If a journey traveler decides to pursue personal holiness, God will make His face known, but there will always be certain "if – then" conditions.

LIFE PRINCIPLE

Today's Life Principle: *Spiritual Divorce.* How do we apply this Life Principle on Day 9? By identifying the **"Top Ten Symptoms of Divorcing God"**:

1. *Spiritual Infidelity* – Have no other god before the Lord God Almighty. He is the God of Abraham, Isaac, and Jacob. He is the God of Israel. There is no other God than Jehovah God.

2. *Absence of Daily Communication with God* – Spend time with God daily. Seek His face, heart and wisdom.

3. *Aberrant Theological Teaching* – Beware of false teaching and aberrant theology. Know your Bible and practice Scriptural principles in life.

4. *Poor Stewardship of One's Time, Talent and Treasure* – God owns everything, even you. You were purchased by the blood of Jesus at Calvary.

5. *Unrepentant Sin* – Jesus said, "*Repent, for the kingdom of heaven is at hand*" (Matthew 4:17b). Repentance is turning from one's sin.

6. *Religion Void of a Relationship* – Religion is easy, but a relationship requires sweat equity – "nothing in nothing out."

7. *Weak Spiritual Foundation* – If your foundation is shaky, don't expect your building to survive when life's earthquakes come.

8. *Addiction to Cultural Norms* – Beware of the temptations of wallowing in the toxic cesspools of ungodly cultural norms. Be washed in the water of the Word of God.

9. *Misplaced Priorities and Fallacious Assumptions* – Live by faith and not by feelings. Feelings change, but God's Word never changes.

10. *Unsaved* – Are you an unrepentant sinner? If so, come to Christ.

LIFE JOURNEY

Personal Life Reflection: What did God say to you today?

_____

_____

_____

_____

_____

_____

_____

The New Journey Prayer using A.C.T.S. (Adoration, Confession, Thanksgiving and Supplication – page 19-20):

1. Are you a humble Christian?
2. Determine this day that you will be a person of genuine humility.
3. Ask the Lord to strengthen you to begin applying the "Fasting Approach: Food Guidelines" on page 243.
4. If you have not been using the "Fasting Approach: Food Guidelines," begin using them throughout the rest of _The New Journey._
5. Add to your prayer list at least three things that you believe will not change unless you commit them to both prayer and fasting.

Fast: **Abstain from eating one meal and practice four hours of absolute silence.**

DAY 10

FOCUS: GOD

Time: _____

Date: _____

Daily Goal:

_____

_____

_____

_____

_____

_____

_____

_____

_____

_____

He's Able

"Any truly repentant
Christian has a right
to full remission
of penalty and
guilt, even without
indulgence letters."

– Martin Luther,
Ninety-five Theses

LIFE STORY

God is Able
Read and Meditate: Ephesians 3:14-21

"Now to Him who is able to do above and beyond all that we ask or think — according to the power that works in us — to Him be glory in the church and in Christ Jesus to all generations, forever and ever. Amen" (Eph. 3:20-21, HCSB).

The Manhunter Martian from Mars, the Green Lantern, Wonder Woman, Superman, Batman, the Flash and Hawkgirl were all members whose chosen role was to squelch evil, crime and known villains hindering justice. I like to think they also fought against godlessness and unrighteousness. Out of all the members of the heroic Justice League, Superman is my favorite. Superman's only nemesis was kryptonite which disabled many, if not all, of Superman's heroic powers. The only force that protected Superman – the Man of Steel – from kryptonite was lead, a natural mineral known only to his new home on Planet Earth. Whenever victimized by kryptonite, Superman immediately learned how to hide beneath a lead fortress as a shield of refuge.

Prayer is our lead fortress and shield of refuge for our souls. God is able to do unbelievable things for us, His people, as long as we humble ourselves beneath the lead fortress of prayer. Sin is the kryptonite that renders our supernatural powers impotent of God's divine enablement.

Do you desire God's power? Is your journey power pack on the brink of a spiritual power outage? Are you attempting to travel on the path to wholeness and holiness while operating on an inadequate spiritual battery? If so, repent of your sin and kneel beneath the lead shield of prayer so God can re-enable the power of prayer in your soul.

LIFE PRINCIPLE

Today's Life Principle: *Confidence in God.* How do we apply this Life Principle on Day 10? We must learn **"God's Devine Pattern"** for how to use His Word in developing confidence in Him: We must *Read, Study, Meditate, Discover and Live* God's Word daily. Let's practice God's Divine Pattern with the following passages:

1. **Numbers 23:19 (NIV):** Balaam said to Balak, "*God is not a man, that He should lie, nor a son of man, that he should change his mind. Does he speak and then not act? Does he promise and not fulfill?*"

2. **Joshua 1:9 (ASV):** The Lord said to Joshua, "*Have not I commanded thee? Be strong and of good courage; be not affrighted, neither be thou dismayed: for Jehovah thy God is with thee whithersoever thou goest.*"

3. **Jeremiah 32:27 (KJV):** The word of the LORD came to Jeremiah, "*Behold, I am the LORD, the God of all flesh: is there any thing too hard for me?*"

4. **Isaiah 41:10 (ESV):** The Lord said, "*Fear not, for I am with you; be not dismayed, for I am your God; I will strengthen you, I will help you, I will uphold you with my righteous right hand.*"

5. **Philippians 4:13 (HCSB):** The Apostle Paul declared to the Philippians, "*I am able to do all things through Him who strengthens me.*"

Never forget, He's able. "*Now to him who is able to do immeasurably more than all we ask or imagine...*" (Ephesians 3:20a, NIV).

LIFE JOURNEY

Personal Life Reflection: What did God say to you today?

_____

_____

_____

_____

_____

_____

_____

_____

The New Journey Prayer using A.C.T.S. (Adoration, Confession, Thanksgiving and Supplication – page 19-20):

1. Identify at least three things in your life God did last year which strengthened you personally, professionally or spiritually.
2. How do you know when your confidence in God is being compromised?
3. Did you pray for your pastor and his family?

Fast: **Abstain from eating one meal and practice four hours of absolute silence.**

DAY 11

FOCUS: GOD

Time: _____

Date: _____

Daily Goal:

_____

_____

_____

_____

_____

_____

_____

_____

_____

_____

The Prayer of Jesus

"Prayer is supposed to have an answer."

– Andrew Murray,
With Christ in the School of Prayer,
p. 31

LIFE STORY

When Jesus Prays, Part 1
Read and Meditate: John 17:1-5

"*These words spake Jesus, and lifted up his eyes to heaven, and said, Father, the hour is come; glorify thy Son, that thy Son also may glorify thee.*" (John 17:1).

"Jimmy is that what you want, baby? Tell mom and she'll get whatever you want. You know mommy and daddy love you. We want you to have everything that we never had. So, sweetheart, just let mommy know what you want and it's yours." Jimmy storms out of the BMW's showroom in Midtown shouting, "Mom! I don't know what I want. Everything I see in the $75,000 to $100,000 price range is the wrong color. I don't even like the color of the tires!" Jimmy jetted out of the BMW's showroom hissing at the renowned Senior International Executive and the number one Sales Consultant in the Eastern United States Region. Jimmy's mother was attempting to honor and promote a son who needed disciplining. Although Jimmy had graduated from Yale University, he remained devoid of simple respect for his parents and professional courtesy for the Executive Consultant.

Jesus, God's One and Only Son, knew how to respect (i.e., honor) His Father. Although He was the Son of God, Second Person of the Godhead, Jesus never disrespected His Father in Heaven. Disrespect diffuses honor, promotion and glory. Jesus knew that if He glorified His Father, His Father would glorify Him. Jesus knew that glory begets glory and honor begets honor. Wholeness and holiness are diffused whenever a son or daughter disrespects their earthly mother or father. Do not expect the reward of God's glory if you refuse to glorify God, the Father in Heaven.

LIFE PRINCIPLE ✕

Today's Life Principle: *Honor.* How do we apply this Life Principle on Day 11? By demonstrating the **"Five Vital Characteristics of a Honorable Person"**:

1. *Honor Both God and Man.* Have an uncanny, God-focused nature. Thirst for the things of God and pursue a ravenous passion to honor the desires of God. God is to be first in life (Matthew 6:33).

2. *Honor All of Humanity.* God created Man in His own image and likeness, both male and female (Genesis 2). Not only understand God's investment in His creation, but equally respect God's rationale. Humanity was God's enterprise, not Man's initiative.

3. *Honor the Value of Being a Motivator.* Motivating others intersects God's redemptive plan of salvation with all humanity. The power of the Holy Spirit motivates our sharing Jesus Christ (Luke 19:10).

4. *Honor the Spirit of Unwavering Perseverance.* The spirit of unwavering perseverance is more than just saying words. It is about the undaunted heart. Refuse to surrender one inch over to the power of Satan. Conclude God is the source of our strength.

5. *Honor the Significance of the Knowledge and Wisdom of God.* Just like a deer pants after water, seek to honor God's wisdom and knowledge. Be unlike the foolish man who says there is no God. Are you a person of honor? Jesus was. He honored and respected His Father.

LIFE JOURNEY

Personal Life Reflection: What did God say to you today?

_____

_____

_____

_____

_____

_____

_____

The New Journey Prayer using A.C.T.S. (Adoration, Confession, Thanksgiving and Supplication – page 19-20):

1. Practice glorifying God today by contacting your church or small group and volunteering to send prayer cards to members who are "Missing in Action."
2. Find a quiet place to pray. Remember you are in a battle with your flesh. Remain committed to the Word of God as you glorify Him. See page 237.
3. When was the last time that you genuinely prayed for your wife, best friend, husband or child?
4. Are you praying for Sunday worship weekly?

Fast: Abstain from eating one meal and practice four hours of absolute silence.

DAY 12

FOCUS: GOD

Time: _____

Date: _____

Daily Goal:

_____

_____

_____

_____

_____

_____

_____

_____

_____

The Prayer of Jesus Continues

"The vital connection between the Word and prayer is one of the simplest and earliest lessons of the Christian life."

– Andrew Murray,
*With Christ in the
School of Prayer,*
p. 175

When Jesus Prays, Part 2
Read and Meditate: John 17:6-19

"Sanctify them by the truth; Your word is truth. As You sent Me into the world, I also have sent them into the world. I sanctify Myself for them, so they also may be sanctified by the truth" (John 17:17-19, HCSB).

Madison was a different kind of a child from birth, but she was not weird. She was uniquely set apart by God. She was intellectually head and shoulders above her peers. She grasped mindboggling concepts with insightful simplicity and self-assurance. Her grandparents often said, "Madison is a gift from Almighty God."

In the same way, Jesus Christ, God's Only Begotten Son, was a gift from God. He too stood head and shoulders above His peers from eternity past to eternity yet to come. He was not simply special, He was God. He was the essence of all truth. He was the way, the truth and the life and no one possessed the power to come to His Father except through His truth (John 14:6). God sanctified Jesus. That is to say, God set Jesus apart to send Him out and bring others back to God the Father. In John 17:6-19, Jesus prayed for Himself. He prayed, *"Sanctify them by the truth; Your word is truth"* (vs. 17).

Jesus' prayer was focused on truth and holiness. It is impossible to be a journey traveler apart from embracing truth and holiness. If we as Christians desire to be head and shoulders above this sinful and fallen world, then we must adhere to "The Prayer of Jesus." Jesus never prayed for us to be taken out of this sinful world, but for us to remain in this sinful world to transform us into the likeness of God. Spiritual transformation begins on our knees in prayer and ends on our face in humble truth and holiness before our Father.

LIFE PRINCIPLE

Today's Life Principle: *Sanctification and Truth.* How do we apply this Life Principle on Day 12? By teaching the **"Seven Requirements of a Life Sanctified by Truth"**:

1. ***Our bodies*** must be living sacrifices unto the Lord Jesus Christ (Romans 12:1-2). Truth is our goal in the sanctification process. The link between sanctification and truth is expressed through the preposition "by." The word "by" is also translated as "through" or "in". We are sanctified by truth, through truth, and in truth. The object of truth is Jesus Christ (John 8). Jesus always demands a sacrifice. Sanctification by truth is impotent when it is without a sacrifice.

2. ***Our souls*** must be fully surrendered to the work of the Lord so our labor in the Lord is not in vain. God demands absolute surrender. There is no other way.

3. ***Our minds*** must be fully released to the mind of Christ (Philippians 2:5). We are not to "mind our own business." We are to mind His business – the business of winning souls (Luke 19:10).

4. ***Our spirits*** must be obedient to the voice of God. *"Hear, O Israel: The LORD our God, the LORD is one"* (Deuteronomy 6:4, ESV). We are to hear then obey respectively.

5. ***Our hearts*** must be committed to the Person of Jesus Christ (Colossians 1:15-20).

6. ***Our wills*** must be enveloped into His will, plan and purpose for our life.

7. ***Our power of prayer*** must not be perfunctorily belching out meaningless words. We must humbly and transparently cry out to our Father for His will to be done.

LIFE JOURNEY

Personal Life Reflection: What did God say to you today?

_____

_____

_____

_____

_____

_____

_____

The New Journey Prayer using A.C.T.S. (Adoration, Confession, Thanksgiving and Supplication – page 19-20):

1. Examine how you are applying truth to your prayer life.
2. Examine how you deal with anger. Refer to pages 246-248.
3. Do you pray truthful prayers? Have you ever truthfully prayed for your worst enemy or adversary?
4. If you don't have an enemy or an adversary, pray for our nation to be a nation of truth and godliness.

Fast: **Abstain from eating one meal, viewing television, listening to secular music, DVD's, CD's, movies and reading emails. Practice absolute silence for two hours.**

DAY 13

FOCUS: GOD

Time: _____

Date: _____

Daily Goal:

_____

_____

_____

_____

_____

_____

_____

_____

_____

The Prayer of Jesus Climax

"God has instituted prayer so as to confer upon His creatures the dignity of being human."

– Blaise Pascal, Richard J. Foster, *Prayer: Finding the Heart's True Home*, p. 229

📖 LIFE STORY

When Jesus Prays, Part 3
Read and Meditate: John 17:20-26

"That they all may be one; as thou, Father, art in me, and I in thee, that they also may be one in us: that the world may believe that thou hast sent me. And the glory which thou gavest me I have given them; that...they may be one, even as we are one: I in them, and thou in me" (John 17:21-23a).

Christopher was his father's one and only son. Frank adored him not only because he was his only son, but he loved Christopher because they were one in the same. At birth Christopher was the mirror image of his father. He possessed the same inherent attributes of his father, Frank. As Christopher grew in wisdom, knowledge and favor with both God and man; his personality beamed with sun-like brilliance. Frank thought to himself, "My son's cheeks are like the radiance of the Aurora Borelis (i.e., Northern Lights) of their native state of Alaska." Frank proudly and purposefully folded his strong arms as he looked at his son from afar, then he took a deep breath and humbly said to himself, "That's my boy! He mirrors my best qualities."

Jesus prayed that all Believers would be mirror images of their Heavenly Father. This oneness with the Father would create unity within the greater Body of Christ – the Church. Yet division remains one of the ugliest blemishes on the face of Christianity. Far too many Christians find it extremely difficult to cooperate as one. Many call this one of the greatest sins of the 21st Century. As Abraham Lincoln said, "A house divided against itself cannot stand." Division weakens us and makes us less effective, less powerful.

What will it take to bring unity back to modern day Christianity? Will it take another program or another new idea from Washington, D.C.? Do we need to pass more legislation? What will it take to remove the gulf of division in modern Christianity? Jesus said, "Prayer." Let us pray that we might be one, not just with the Father, but with each other as well.

LIFE PRINCIPLE

Today's Life Principle: *Oneness.* How do we apply this Life Principle on Day 13? By practicing the **"Five Restoration Elements of a Repentant Church"**:

1. *Intellectual Element:* Oneness with the Father begins with our thinking. As a man thinks, so he is. One must aggressively pursue oneness as an ongoing goal for community living in the body of Christ.

2. *Emotional Element:* Oneness with the Father is often more emotional than intellectual. Being emotional does not suggest grotesque emotional releases. We are emotional and intellectual beings and God still speaks to us through our hearts and minds. He desires our human sensitivity and our intellectual participation as we seek oneness in Christ's Body – the Church.

3. *Volitional Element:* Oneness is equally volitional. Ignoring our own volitional element is to extinguish any possibility of authentic, Christ-centered oneness with God and Man. The volitional element addresses one's personal will. When we surrender our will over to the will of Almighty God, we exercise personal choice or free will. Do we honestly want to develop a oneness-centered church community or do we prefer perpetual division and sinful individualism?

4. *Transformational:* Transformation is deeply connected to one's volition. Volition deals with man whereas transformation involves God. Only God can make us one. Only God can change us.

5. *Evangelistic Element:* A repentant church will seek ways to share Christ daily in the same way as a repentant saint. Are you a repentant saint?

LIFE JOURNEY

Personal Life Reflection: What did God say to you today?

_____

_____

_____

_____

_____

_____

_____

The New Journey Prayer using A.C.T.S. (Adoration, Confession, Thanksgiving and Supplication – page 19-20):

1. Oneness with the Father begins with _____
    _____ (*write your name in the space*).
2. Examine what anxiety does to limit or depreciate oneness with the Father. Refer to pages 249-250.
3. Are you a force for unity or division in your church? Be honest.
4. Are you praying for your pastor and the leaders of your church family?
5. Have you fasted at least one time on *The New Journey*?

Fast: Abstain from eating one meal, viewing television, listening to secular music, DVD's, CD's, movies or reading emails. Practice absolute silence for two hours.

DAY 14

FOCUS: GOD

Time: _____

Date: _____

Daily Goal:

_____

_____

_____

_____

_____

_____

_____

_____

_____

_____

Prayer at Midnight

"Sanctification is both a step of faith and a process of works."

– Hannah Whitall Smith, *The Christian's Secret of a Happy Life*, p. 17

LIFE STORY

Answered Prayer at Midnight
Read and Meditate: Acts 16:25-34

"And at midnight Paul and Silas prayed, and sang praises unto God: and the prisoners heard them. And suddenly there was a great earthquake, so that the foundations of the prison were shaken: and immediately all the doors were opened, and every one's bands were loosed" (Acts 16:25-26).

Daniel David Maxwell was charismatic, energetic, intelligent and an Ivy League Academic All American from Yale University. He was known as the "Golden Boy." Then came a midnight knock at the door that threw a blanket of fear over the Maxwell home like thick London fog.

"Mr. and Mrs. Maxwell," the head coach's voice cracked, "Daniel David has been injured. I'm here to drive you to the hospital." As they drove to the hospital, the Maxwell's were praying, "Heavenly Father, have mercy, Lord!" The Maxwell's continued steadfastly in their prayers and God answered. As they arrived at the emergency entrance with the coach, Daniel David miraculously met them at the door. No bruises or scratches were on him. What appeared to be a life-threatening injury was nothing more than a minor concussion. The doctor approached them in utter amazement and said, "He was not breathing. Then within a flash while on the gurney, he sat up and smiled. In my 20 years of medical practice, I have never witnessed anything like this before. Your son went from death to life."

God answers prayer. So, let us continue to **PUSH** – Pray Until Something **H**appens. Paul and Silas "pushed" and God delivered them from a Roman jail in the city of Philippi. They found freedom in prison at midnight.

LIFE PRINCIPLE

Today's Life Principle: *Steadfastness.* How do we apply this Life Principle on Day 14? By using the **"Seven Ingredients in a Steadfast Prayer Life"**:

1. *Courage*: Courage allows us to deal with insurmountable problems and satanic attacks.

2. *Commitment*: We need a deeper commitment to God while addressing problems. A successful resolution apart from God's divine intervention is not possible.

3. *Confidence*: We need a richer confidence in God the Father. He is able to help us in our times of need if we remain steadfast in our prayer life.

4. *Calling*: We need to be divinely called by the Spirit of God to remain steadfast in our prayer life until God answers.

5. *Experience.* We need to experience true companionship with God on a daily basis in our steadfast prayers.

6. *Knowledge.* We need to know how to commune with our God, the Holy Spirit, on a daily basis through our prayer life.

7. *Sharing.* We need to share Jesus as Savior and Lord to a lost, dying and sinful world.

A steadfast prayer life is a privilege and a prize from God. God desires to hear from His children. Praying steadfastly is learning how to live life at the door of the empty tomb. There is no need for us to allow midnight to limit our faithful and determined prayer life. It has been said, "Life without prayer is like death without knowing it." God honors the steadfast prayer life of all Believers. He wants us to pray. He desires we never allow our circumstances to dictate our prayer life.

LIFE JOURNEY

Personal Life Reflection: What did God say to you today?

_____

_____

_____

_____

_____

_____

_____

The New Journey Prayer using A.C.T.S. (Adoration, Confession, Thanksgiving and Supplication – page 19-20):

1. Paul and Silas displayed no signs of bitterness or unforgiveness even while they were in a Philippian jail. Study "The Six Tools of Dealing with Unforgiveness" on pages 251-252.
2. Are you on the verge of a divorce or a marital separation?
3. Do you practice unforgiveness or forgiveness?
4. Determine to practice steadfastness when it comes to overcoming major injustices that occur in your relationships.
5. Are you keeping a daily prayer list?

Fast: **Abstain from eating one meal, viewing television, listening to secular music, DVD's, CD's, movies or reading emails. Practice absolute silence for two hours.**

DAY 15

FOCUS: GOD

Time: _____

Date: _____

Daily Goal:

_____

_____

_____

_____

_____

_____

_____

_____

_____

_____

Earnest Prayer

"Unceasing prayer has a way of speaking peace to the chaos."

– Richard J. Foster, *Prayer: Finding the Heart's True Home*, p. 121

LIFE STORY

Earnest Prayer in the Church
Read and Meditate: Acts 12:5-18

"Peter therefore was kept in prison: but prayer was made without ceasing of the church unto God for him" (Acts 12:5).

Mary was the mother of a son who had lost his way. Ben was incarcerated for a crime he did not commit. Although the evidence was circumstantial, the courts convicted him and shipped him off to an Illinois prison. Ben's mother believed in the power of prayer. She not only was the executive secretary for her church's senior pastor, but she was also her church's intercessory prayer ministry coordinator. For several years she encouraged the church to pray (Matthew 7:7). Mary's philosophy was "Prayer and God work hand-in-hand. Prayer tells God what's on our minds and God directs prayer to do what's on His mind."

The Church was not concerned with the power of Herod and his Roman authorities. God possesses the power of divine intervention when it comes to delivering His people. Earnest prayer offered up by the church literally plucked Peter, sleeping between two soldiers, out of prison and placed him knocking at the door of a church-wide intercessory prayer meeting. Rhoda heard the knocking, hurried to the door and saw Peter. She notified the prayer warriors that Peter was actually at the door. Unfortunately, their disbelief disregarded Rhoda's announcement. Rhoda was persistent. Peter really was at the door. God answers all prayers either "yes", "no" or "not now." He responds to earnest prayers prayed from earnest hearts.

LIFE PRINCIPLE

Today's Life Principle: *Persistence.* How do we apply this Life Principle on Day 15? It is achieved through persistence in establishing a Standing in the Gap Prayer Ministry for the local church. There are **"Four Relational Circles of a Standing in the Gap Church Prayer Ministry"** (refer to Acts 1:8):

1. *Jerusalem:* The Church's first assignment is to boldly petition the throne of grace and mercy for those residing in our "Jerusalem." Jerusalem is where family, friends and close loved ones reside. Jerusalem was the first church plant and home of the Gospel. To overlook home and leap to Judea is a grave error. We must start at home with the Gospel, and then branch out to the next three relational prayer circles.

2. *Judea:* "Judea" is our place of influence and relationship – our neighborhoods, communities, business partners and employment relationships. The Gospel is needed here as well. These relationships are predicated by our environment. These are people we work with, talk to, as well as encounter in various situations.

3. *Samaria:* "Samaria" is a more distant place of relationships. Samaria is our city, state and nation. Planting the Gospel in Samaria encompasses all types of businesses, religious institutions, organizations, political parties, etc.

4. *Uttermost:* Planting uttermost prayer is our world at large. Uttermost prayer cries out to God for the whole o f humanity. It is our prayers spanning the globe.

LIFE JOURNEY

Personal Life Reflection: What did God say to you today?

_____

_____

_____

_____

_____

_____

_____

The New Journey Prayer using A.C.T.S. (Adoration, Confession, Thanksgiving and Supplication – page 19-20):

1. Do you give up quickly?
2. Pray to God that you will be more determined and persistent as a Christian.
3. Pray that more and more Christians will demonstrate an unparalleled persistence in practicing the spiritual disciplines of prayer, fasting and reading God's Word.

Fast: **Abstain from eating one meal, viewing television, listening to secular music, DVD's, CD's, movies and reading emails. Practice absolute silence for two hours.**

DAY 16

FOCUS: GOD

Time: _____

Date: _____

Daily Goal:

_____

_____

_____

_____

_____

_____

_____

_____

_____

_____

In the Fish's Belly

"No man-made gauge can measure the shock and horror that strike the nervous system as ill-fated news travels into the human ear."

– Charles R. Swindoll, *Seasons of Life*, p. 91

LIFE STORY

A Prayer Meeting in the Belly of a Fish
Read and Meditate: Jonah 2:1-10

"Then Jonah prayed unto the LORD his God out of the fish's belly…"
(Jonah 2:1).

Zoe and Butch got engaged at the age of 18. They were high school sweethearts. Butch was drafted into the military and served in Vietnam for four years. On the day Butch arrived home from Nam, he married Zoe. The following year Grace Nicole was born. Immediately Butch and Zoe began having serious marital problems. Butch was drinking heavily and Zoe was sliding into deep depression. Butch realized that things were literally falling apart and, in a moment of desperation, he cried out, "Lord, God where are You? I'm losing my way, Father. My wife is drowning in the deepest pit of emotional depression. Lord, God of Heaven and Earth, please save us now."

In the same way, Jonah cried out to the "Lord, God" from within the belly of the big fish. Out of anger and utter frustration, Jonah accused the Lord, God of casting him into a hopeless deep. Jonah paints a vivid picture of his demise. Death had wrapped its tentacles around him like sea weed. Jonah's hope appeared to have lost its usefulness; it began to sink into the bottomless pit of the sea.

Paul writes, *"And hope does not disappoint us…"* (Romans 5:5a, NIV). Like Jonah, Butch and Zoe eventually learned the value of hope that refuses to let down even the most disappointed Believer. Every Believer can have a prayer meeting, even in the belly of monster troubles.

LIFE PRINCIPLE 🛠

Today's Life Principle: *Hope.* How do we apply this Life Principle on Day 16? In desperate times, the **"Three Unusual Places to Discover Eternal Hope"** are in:

1. *Hidden Places:* Hope is all around us. It is everywhere. We must be attuned to harmonizing our spiritual senses with the supernatural insight and wisdom of God. God knows no hidden places. He sees and understands all things. Generations may come and go, but the human eye will never be able to perceive what God knew before the course of time. We must learn to hide out in God's secret place of prayer. There we will discover the blessings and benefits of uncovering the daily joy of hidden places.

2. *Hard Places:* Difficulties are often a sign of being in a hard place. Hard places are where the womb of God produces new, luscious health and vivacious, life-sustaining fruit. Our spiritual fruit grows from abiding in Christ (John 15). The harder the place, the more nourishing and flavorful is the fruit. Fruit is what the common man desires most, but if this is all he seeks, he will not find it. Instead he will find himself in a hard place. Remember, hard places are not designed to hinder our hope. They are designed to harness our hope and store it for times when we are stricken with the leprosy of hopelessness. Hard places allow us to prepare for hard times. So, store up your hope in Christ and you will flourish eternally when the hard times come.

3. *Hurting Places:* Hope is often discovered in hurting places. No one seeks hope in such places, but they are often the best place to discover the purest and most precious kind of hope. The deeper the hurt, the more rooted our hope can become. This is the kind of hope that will last eternally. Butch and Jonah both discovered where to find hope in unusual places. Have you discovered such a place of hope for your soul?

LIFE JOURNEY

Personal Life Reflection: What did God say to you today?

_____

_____

_____

_____

_____

_____

_____

The New Journey Prayer using A.C.T.S. (Adoration, Confession, Thanksgiving and Supplication – page 19-20):

1. Identify people in your church and community who have served in the military. Develop a prayer list of needs in their life.

2. Ask God to help you start a monthly _New Journey_ Small Group Prayer Ministry with friends, associates and family members. Refer to pages 185-202.

3. How long is your prayer list? Are you being faithful to pray for each individual on your prayer list?

Fast: Abstain from eating three meals and practice absolute silence for eight hours.

DAY 17

FOCUS: GOD

Time: _____

Date: _____

Daily Goal:

_____

_____

_____

_____

_____

_____

_____

_____

_____

Look Like Christ

"The earnestness that we work up in the energy of the flesh is a repulsive thing. The earnestness created in us by the Holy Spirit if pleasing to God."

– R. A. Torrey, *Power-Filled Living: How to Receive God's Best for Your Life*, p. 290

LIFE STORY

Learning to Look Like Christ
Read and Meditate: Ephesians 5:1-2

"Therefore, be imitators of God," (Ephesians 5:1a, HCSB).

Often criticized for living in the shadow of his father, Samuel Thomas Strong, Sr., "Little Sam" lived a frustrated life. "Little Sam," Professor Sanford said, "You are just like your father." He had graduated from the same high school, Christian college and seminary as his father. Little Sam didn't appreciate being in the shadow of his father. He began to learn he was his own person and grew to realize God had made him uniquely different. Little Sam was his own man. He was his father's son, but he was his own person.

Christ-likeness is no different. As Christians, we are not Christ. We are to be like Christ. The word "like" suggests possessing similar qualities while remaining unique and independent. Christians are like Christ, not Christ in human flesh. Paul never demanded the Ephesians become carbon copies of him, but be like the Christ in him. Paul admonished them to live as dearly loved children walking in the ways of Christ.

Years passed and Little Sam overcame living in his father's shadow. He began to appreciate his unique qualities and learned how to be his own man beyond the shadow of his father. When Little Sam's father died, he was called to pastor his father's church. He took the church through three building programs and grew the church to 5,000 in 20 years. Little Sam learned how to imitate his father without being a carbon copy of his father.

LIFE PRINCIPLE

Today's Life Principle: *Imitators.* How do we apply this Life Principle on Day 17? It is accomplished through becoming imitators of Christ. **"The 4 B's for Becoming an Imitator of Christ"** are:

1. **Be Real:** It is difficult to catch people being who they really are. The world promotes carbon copies and copy cats. God made each of us though as originals. When we are who God created us to be, we are truly being ourselves. Make it a personal endeavor to be real, with warts and quirks smeared all over. Once we are real with ourselves, then we can become real with God and Man. When we learn to live life in the real zone, we will embrace what it means to be imitators of Christ.

2. **Be Relational:** The Christian "Lone Ranger" does not imitate Christ. Christ calls us into community as members of the Body of Christ. Relational ministry begins with our perception of the character of God. The more authentic our relationship with God, the more fluid our relationships will be with others.

3. **Be Radical:** God calls each of us to become radical Christ followers. Are we radical or do we do radical things? Things like forgiving those who refuse to forgive us or loving those who refuse to love us. Do we encourage those who discourage us and bless those who curse us? Radical love requires doing radical things.

4. **Be Right:** Being right does not make us right with God. Far too many of us seek to be right with each other while floundering over the most crucial right, being right with God. It is impossible to be right with Man when we are not right with God. Being right with God is always first (Matthew 6:33).

LIFE JOURNEY

Personal Life Reflection: What did God say to you today?

_____

_____

_____

_____

_____

_____

_____

The New Journey Prayer using A.C.T.S. (Adoration, Confession, Thanksgiving and Supplication – page 19-20):

1. Do you know anyone who practices imitating Christ daily? Pray for that person because he or she will come under satanic attack at some point.
2. Pray that you will imitate Christ daily.
3. As a Christian who is seeking to imitate Christ, pray for persons who are dealing with spiritual strongholds in their life and/or family. Study the Scriptures on "Breaking Spiritual Strongholds" on page 244. Take a moment and pray for them.

Fast: **Abstain from eating three meals and practice absolute silence for eight hours.**

DAY 18

FOCUS: GOD

Time: _____

Date: _____

Daily Goal:

_____

_____

_____

_____

_____

_____

_____

_____

_____

Maturing on the Journey

"Unfortunately, blind spots affect more than cars. All of us have personal blind spots."

– Bill McCartney, *Blind Spots*, p. 7

Maturing on the Journey to Wholeness and Holiness
Read and Meditate: Ephesians 4:14-16

"Then we will no longer be little children, tossed by the waves and blown around by every wind of teaching, by human cunning with cleverness in the techniques of deceit. But speaking the truth in love, let us grow in every way into Him who is the head — Christ" (Eph. 4:14-15, HCSB).

Jerri graduated with honors, but her parents had given up on her. She did everything the hard way. If it was simple, Jerri could find the most difficult way to achieve the task. She made simple things difficult and difficult things impossible. Until one day when Jerri crashed headlong into the proverbial wall of human reality. That was the day Jerri became a mature, young adult. Her parents were perplexed. They asked, "What happened to you? Are you ill? Did you do some dim-witted thing we are soon to hear of tomorrow?" "No, all is well," said Jerri. "I've just decided to stop acting like a two-year-old. I have grown up."

The New Journey to Wholeness and Holiness requires spiritual maturity. Infantile religion is antiquated. Mature Christians seek to operate in the perfect will of God as opposed to His permissive will. God's perfect will implies what God prefers for us, while God's permissive will implies what God permits us to do: *Perfect Will* – Divine Choice; *Permissive Will* – Divine Allowance. The mark of a mature Christian is conveyed through the words of Paul, *"Then we will no longer be little children"* (Eph. 4:14, NIV). Mature Christians grow up and graduate, but immature Christians may never graduate into spiritual maturity.

LIFE PRINCIPLE ✖

Today's Life Principle: *Maturity.* How do we apply this Life Principle on Day 18? By achieving the **"Nine Marks of Godly Christian Character"**:

1. *Looks:* Realize that physical looks have nothing to do with inner beauty (Proverbs 31). Focus not on external beauty, but on godly character.

2. *Likes:* Like what God likes. Adopt this philosophy: "If God is not in it or supporting it, then it's not for me." Know where God is at work and join Him (Henry Blackaby, *Experiencing God*).

3. *Language:* Use the tongue to glorify God. Be purposeful with any speech. Do not use words without weighing them on the righteous scales of God's supernatural wisdom and insight. Consult with God before communicating with Man.

4. *Lifestyle:* Do not be impressed with today's lifestyles, fashions and Hollywood images. Refuse to worship image consultants. Our lifestyle coach is the Holy Spirit of God. Consult the Counselor before communicating any thoughts. Realize life is more than keeping up with today's styles.

5. *Lust:* Lust for more of God, more prayer, more fellowship with other believers, more life in Christ and more opportunities to make Christ known.

6. *Listening Skills:* Listen to learn God's will.

7. *Leverage:* Leverage love and compassion.

8. *Lures:* Help others untangle the lures of ungodliness in their lives. Use the only lure–love for God.

9. *Love:* Understand love is the most excellent way. Love at all cost.

LIFE JOURNEY

Personal Life Reflection: What did God say to you today?

_____

_____

_____

_____

_____

_____

_____

The New Journey Prayer using A.C.T.S. (Adoration, Confession, Thanksgiving and Supplication – page 19-20):

1. Ask God to teach you how to practice operating in the perfect will of God as opposed to the permissive will of God.
2. Examine how you use your tongue as a maturing Christian. Refer to pages 253-255, "Tools for Dealing with the Tongue."
3. Pray and ask the Lord Jesus Christ to give you a new tongue.
4. Examine whether you ever gossip or if there is gossip in your church? If so, pray and fast.
5. How many days have you fasted as instructed in _The New Journey_?

Fast: Abstain from eating two meals, viewing television for 24 hours and attending secular movies.

DAY 19

FOCUS: GOD

Time: _____

Date: _____

Daily Goal:

_____

_____

_____

_____

_____

_____

_____

_____

_____

Be Real

"What's the cure for selfishness? Get your self out of your eye by getting your eye off your self. Quit staring at that little self, and focus on your great Savior."

– Max Lucado,
Grace for the Moment, Vol. II,
p. 30

LIFE STORY

Be Real and Speak the Truth
Read and Meditate: Ephesians 4:25

"Since you put away lying, Speak the truth, each one to his neighbor, because we are members of one another" (Eph. 4:25, HCSB).

Jesus said, *"And ye shall know the truth, and the truth shall make you free"* (John 8:32) and *"I am the way, the truth, and the life: no man cometh unto the Father, but by me"* (John 14:6b). Jesus frequently parallels truth with freedom which leads to personal deliverance and individual authenticity.

Nate was an atrocious, habitual liar. Even when he sought to speak truthfully, lies almost always were substituted with more lies. One day, Nate's childhood best friend was diagnosed with cancer. Since Bill had been sedated to complete his diagnostic examination, Bill's wife was too afraid to inform him of the doctor's prognosis. Sarah called Nate to assist her in breaking the sensitive news to Bill. Since, Nate was a habitual liar for more than 30 years, would Bill believe his friend and take his words seriously?

Paul is right on target when he writes, *"...put away lying, Speak the truth, each one to his neighbor, because we are members of one another."* Truth liberates while lies incarcerate. After much prayer, Nate was able to speak truthfully to Bill by the grace of God. Nate was equipped in a way that amazed his friends how he presented the truth to Bill. This one act of truth saved Bill's life and changed Nate's as well. From that day forward, Nate became known as a truth teller.

LIFE PRINCIPLE

Today's Life Principle: *Truth.* How do we apply this Life Principle on Day 19? Why is it so difficult for a Christian to speak truth in love? Because there are **"Five Deadliest Lies About the Truth"**:

1. ***Truth Hurts:*** This is one of the most flagrant lies that seek to contaminate the purity of truth. The truth will sting from time to time, but truth in love never injures. There are also times when truth crushes prideful, arrogant hearts and smashes ancient myths or fleshly human wisdom. Truth strikes the bulls-eye, but it heals instead of kills.

2. ***Truth Divides:*** Truth never divides but it does separate. Truth separates good from evil, right from wrong, and the spirit of Satan from the Spirit of the Savior. The truth and a lie will never occupy the same place both physically and spiritually once the Light of God shines (Matthew 5:13-16).

3. ***Truth Fails:*** Truth never fails. The only way truth *seems* to fail is when a half-truth is presented out of the mouth of a liar. A half-truth is when a lie is concealed beneath a cloak that looks like truth. Regardless of how we dress it, a lie is still a lie and a sin.

4. ***Truth is Relative:*** It has been said, "My truth is my truth and your truth is your truth." This is another lie from the demon of darkness – the Devil. Truth is a constant and not a variable. Truth does not change (John 8). Truth will always survive the test of time. Always speak the truth in love because truth always prevails.

5. ***Truth Is Impersonal:*** Wrong! Truth is a Person. That person is none other than the Lord, Jesus Christ. Jesus said, "*I am the way, the truth...*" Live truth as we speak truth. Practice what we speak.

LIFE JOURNEY

Personal Life Reflection: What did God say to you today?

_____

_____

_____

_____

_____

_____

_____

The New Journey Prayer using A.C.T.S. (Adoration, Confession, Thanksgiving and Supplication – page 19-20):

1. Pray that you will be a person who speaks the truth in love.

2. How are you doing with your tongue today? Examine how you used your tongue as a maturing Christian yesterday. Refer to pages 253-255, "Tools for Dealing with the Tongue."

3. Was there any improvement? If so, stop and thank God. If not, confess to God and repent.

Fast: Abstain from eating two meals, viewing television for 24 hours and attending secular movies.

DAY 20

FOCUS: GOD

Time: _____

Date: _____

Daily Goal:

_____

_____

_____

_____

_____

_____

_____

_____

_____

Be Angry, Sin Not

"Portraits of hurt will be replaced by landscapes of grace. Walls of anger will be demolished and shaky foundations restored."

– Max Lucado, *Everyday Blessings*, p. 276

LIFE STORY

Be Angry but Sin Not
Read and Meditate: Ephesians 4:26-27

"Be angry and do not sin. Don't let the sun go down on your anger, and don't give the Devil an opportunity" (Eph. 4:26-27, HCSB).

His fist penetrated the sheetrock wall in the family room as if it were a thin veneer of Styrofoam. Why was Joe so angry? What was it that pushed him over the edge? Joe's invited guests were paralyzed with fear. They had never seen Joe like this. Joe's classmates decided to confront him. With tears in his eyes and shame on his face, Joe begged forgiveness, "Please forgive me. I just lost my job today." Instead of attacking Joe, his friends decided to blanket him with prayer. As the prayers went up as a sweet smelling aroma to the Lord, Joe fell to his knees and cried out in a gentle voice, "Heavenly Father, please help."

June Hunt, best-selling Christian writer, understood Joe's anger. She believes that anger is not altogether wrong. Hunt wants people to ask the question, "Why am I angry?" Anger becomes destructive only when it is out of control. When it is under the control of the Holy Spirit of God, anger can produce positive results. God often uses our anger to glorify Himself.

Paul asserts, "In your anger do not sin." If you are a person of uncontrollable, explosive anger, learn the value of prayer. Pray to God to blanket you with inner peace and envelop you with internal control. When angry, do not sin. We can overcome anger as we submit to the power of the Holy Spirit. God is waiting to hear from us. We must learn to seek God's divine intervention daily so when we are angry, we do not sin. Godless anger lures and lies. Righteous anger leads and liberates.

LIFE PRINCIPLE

Today's Life Principle: *Anger.* How do we apply this Life Principle on Day 20? It is achieved through revealing the **"Five Positive Sides to Anger"**:

1. *Anger Protects:* Anger often serves as a valiant protector. It is a watch guard between light and darkness. Anger takes its position beside us and alerts us to oncoming dangers. These dangers are often unseen forces of evil and unheard satanic attacks coming up from the underworld. Anger is the fire of God in our belly used to ward off satanic attacks and disperse forces of evil in high places (Eph. 6:10-20). God says, "*Be angry but sin not*" (Eph. 4:26-27, HCSB).

2. *Anger Purifies:* Anger also has medicinal purposes. Anger not only sanctifies, it equally purifies. It removes all the unwholesome contaminants from within the inner sanctuary of the believer's soul. Anger reminds us as Christians that we are no better than the lowest of sinners. As we learn to control our anger, it purifies our hearts and minds with a new level of thinking. We are now being controlled by the Spirit of God.

3. *Anger Purges:* Anger purges the human soul. It removes what ought not to be and replaces it with what God desires. Learning how to allow God to clean out our impure anger is key to Christian maturity.

4. *Anger Points:* All *New Journey* travelers possess anger triggers or hot spots. We must at all times beware of our hot spots. This is how we can successfully manage our anger.

5. *Anger Pleases:* One of the most perplexing things about anger is that it pleases God if it is righteous anger. We have the right to become angry over sin – yet sin not.

Praise God for learning how to apply each of the right sides of anger.

 **LIFE JOURNEY**

Personal Life Reflection: What did God say to you today?

_____

_____

_____

_____

_____

_____

_____

The New Journey Prayer using A.C.T.S. (Adoration, Confession, Thanksgiving and Supplication – page 19-20):

1. Are you an angry person? Do you yell at your spouse and kids? When was the last time you told your spouse of your sincere love?
2. Do you believe God can heal you of your anger?
3. Ask God to teach you how to control your anger and heal your soul this day.
4. Meditate on "The 13 Tools for Dealing with Anger" on pages 246-248.
5. Pray to the Lord for anger control.

Fast: **Abstain from eating two meals, viewing television for 24 hours and attending secular movies.**

DAY 21

FOCUS: GOD

Time: _____

Date: _____

Daily Goal:

_____

_____

_____

_____

_____

_____

_____

_____

_____

Be Honest

"God wants more than slavish obedience from us, He wants to change us. G. K. Chesterton once wrote, 'Virtue is not just the absence of vices or the avoidance of moral dangers; virtue is a vivid and separate thing."

– Terry Glaspey,
C. S. Lewis: His Life & Thoughts, p. 124

LIFE STORY

Be Honest and Don't Steal
Read and Meditate: Ephesians 4:28

"The thief must no longer steal. Instead, he must do honest work with his own hands, so that he has something to share with anyone in need" (Eph. 4:28, HCSB).

How can a dishonest man serve God in genuine honesty? Dishonesty should never be the norm when it comes to Kingdom service. A man's position is devoid of truth when there is a thievish nature of dishonesty and irreverence to God. One's honest position with God must always follow the pattern of a personal relationship with Jesus Christ.

For Nathan, salvation always preceded Christian service. He believed that once you possess a personal relationship with Jesus Christ, Christian service must overshadow fleshly dishonesty to avoid division, disharmony and disaster. Nathan knew honesty was one of the precious fruits of righteousness, but dishonesty was a poisonous fruit growing out of unrighteousness. Our hands always follow our heart. When the heart is right with God, the hands will work to honor God's Son, the Lord Jesus Christ. Nathan's heart was right and honest.

Ephesians is about "putting shoe leather to the Gospel" and learning how to live what we profess to believe. Nathan believed "Behavior should always mirror belief." We must avoid thievish living by steering clear of stealing and dishonesty. God delights when we deny self while embracing the Savior. Godly character is never the objective of an unrepentant thief. As a child of God, continue to grow and mature in truth. Surrender your all this day. Truthfully abide in Christ (John 15:7-8) and be real.

LIFE PRINCIPLE

Today's Life Principle: *Behavior Mirrors Belief.* How do we apply this Life Principle on Day 21? It is achieved through realizing that how we behave is an expression of what we truly believe. **"Ten Ways Our Behavior Mirrors Our Belief"** are:

1. *Our Talk:* The way we talk communicates what we truly believe.
2. *Our Walk:* The way we walk tells the world who we are. Our "walk" lifestyle. It is about how we live as Christians.
3. *Our Dress:* Christian dress ought to honor God. When it does not, it becomes a window into the inner life of one's soul.
4. *Our Service:* Christian service is about serving God and Man with great joy.
5. *OurWorship:* Christian worship implies putting God first. God delights and demands our worship (Psalm 150).
6. *Our Love:* Christian love is about sacrifice and surrender. Sacrifice to God and surrender to His perfect will.
7. *Our Prayer:* Saying words is not saying prayers. Simply praying words does not reflect having a genuine, mature prayer life. Prayer is an on-going conversation with God.
8. *Our Forgiveness:* Christian forgiveness is more than saying, "I'm sorry." It is about the giving of self to restore a healthy, productive nearness with one's fellow man.
9. *Our Look:* An angry, contorted face is a picture of what lurks within our soul, despite our public persona or professional image. Our exterior countenance should reflect our inner, Christian peace.
10. *Our Death:* Death should never cause fear. When we die as Christians, it should be a time of great celebration. Death is Christian's door to eternal life.

LIFE JOURNEY

Personal Life Reflection: What did God say to you today?

_____

_____

_____

_____

_____

_____

_____

The New Journey Prayer using A.C.T.S. (Adoration, Confession, Thanksgiving and Supplication – page 19-20):

1. How are you doing on *The New Journey*? Do you sense any change in your life?
2. If there is no change in your life at this stage, try fasting this day. Don't rob yourself of blessings awaiting you.
3. Malachi 3:8a says, "Will a man rob God?" Are you robbing God not only of tithes and offerings, but also in faithful service to God and man? Pause now and pray for change in your life.
4. Commit today to make your behavior mirror your belief. If your behavior does not match your belief as a Christian, refer to pages 203-224 and consider fasting.

Fast: **Abstain from eating two meals, viewing television for 24 hours and attending secular movies.**

DAY 22

FOCUS: GOD

Time: _____

Date: _____

Daily Goal:

_____

_____

_____

_____

_____

_____

_____

_____

_____

Mouth Cleaning

"He who has a sharp tongue soon cuts his own throat."

– E. C. McKenzie, *Quips & Quotes*, p. 518

LIFE STORY

Clean Out Your Mouth
Read and Meditate: Ephesians 4:29

"No rotten talk should come from your mouth, but only what is good for the building up of someone in need, in order to give grace to those who hear" (Eph. 4:29, HCSB).

In the southern most side of Gloria's hometown was the municipal sanitary landfill. Trash was trucked in from several adjoining counties. In its heyday, the Smith County Municipal Sanitary Landfill was an industrial marvel. However, today it is the stench and shame of the entire region. For several years a multi-county regional commission has engaged in a feasibility study to determine the next steps – either correct the problem or abandon the 50 year old landfill and start from scratch with a new design and regional commission. If the local officials fail to address the stench, then thousands of citizens threaten to either file a petition to Hazardous Waste Management Commission or vote the leadership out of office.

The apostle Paul, in his letter to the believers in the region of Ephesus, addressed a similar type of stench – rotten talk. Paul knew that rotten talk contaminates and stifles the effectiveness of the Lord's work. An unmanaged human tongue must be spiritually addressed by the Body of Christ. Wholeness and holiness cannot be achieved when spiritual leaders refuse to address the root of the human problem – unrepentant sin. Once unrepentant sin is addressed, disgrace is removed and the work of Christ lunges forward. Therefore, *"Do not let any unwholesome talk come out of your mouths ..."* (Ephesians 4:29, NIV). Let us learn to keep our mouths clean.

LIFE PRINCIPLE

Today's Life Principle: *Leadership.* How do we apply this Life Principle on Day 22? By learning how godly Christian leadership impacts the local church. There are **"Five Impacts of a Godly Christian Leader"**:

1. *Church Health*: Godly leadership directly impacts the health of the Lord's Church. A healthy church often gets that way through strong, godly leadership. Although unhealthy churches can grow rapidly, the unhealthy growth usually will not last. While healthy church growth may take years, it will last.

2. *Church Holiness*: Holiness has to do with being set apart by God for better service. Holiness is about cleansing and removing anything which hinders the freedom of the Holy Spirit from achieving His awesome work by His divine leadership.

3. *Church Work*: The work of the church is to seek and to save the lost (Luke 19:10). Redeeming the lost, restoring the backslidden and reviving the saved are the ultimate works of the Lord's Church (Romans 1, 3, 6, 8, 12).

4. *Church Wealth*: Church wealth is not simply about focusing on money. A healthy, wealthy church is one that seeks to help others. As the church helps others, the Lord continues to reinvest back into His Church for future opportunities. Someone has said, "Nothing going in, nothing coming out."

5. *Church Witness*: The word "witness" means "martyr." A martyr is one who gives one's life for a cause. Godly leadership always calls the Body of Christ to martyr to ourselves for the evangelization of lost and hurting souls. Godly leadership teaches us, as martyrs in the Body, to never be ashamed of the Gospel (Rom. 1:16).

LIFE JOURNEY

Personal Life Reflection: What did God say to you today?

_____

_____

_____

_____

_____

_____

_____

The New Journey Prayer using A.C.T.S. (Adoration, Confession, Thanksgiving and Supplication – page 19-20):

1. Do you know any Christian, including yourself, who has difficulty controlling the tongue? Refer to page 253 and study Proverbs 10:19; 12:18; 17:28; 21:13 and Eph. 4:29-30 to assist in your battle with the tongue and ministering to others.
2. Begin praying for people you know who have been wounded by an unbridled tongue. Refer to the "Prayer Disciples Prayer List" on pages 259-260 and pray for them by name. You are free to make multiple copies from _The New Journey_ for your prayer ministry.

Fast: Abstain from eating one meal.

DAY 23

FOCUS: GOD

Time: _____

Date: _____

Daily Goal:

_____

_____

_____

_____

_____

_____

_____

_____

_____

_____

The Heart Matters

"Violence is the ugliest fruit."

– Max Lucado,
A Love Worth Giving Living in the Overflow of God's Love, p. 38

LIFE STORY

The Heart Matters: Be Kind to Each Other and Forgive in Christ
Read and Meditate: Ephesians 4:32

"And be kind and compassionate to one another, forgiving one another, just as God also forgave you in Christ" (Eph. 4:32, HCSB).

As a Harvard Law School graduate, Johnny was taught that kindness, compassion and forgiveness were signs of a weak-hearted lawyer. He was taught to bluntly and belligerently argue his case with all his heart, regardless of the feelings of others. He was told that if you are going to succeed professionally as a strong-hearted lawyer, then boldly plow over your opponent without humility or mercy. His head was filled with this philosophy. Johnny returned home with a hard heart and a stubborn head. To those who did not know him, he appeared to be the typical calloused and arrogant Harvard attorney. One day Aaron, his hometown's best friend, said. "What happened to you at Harvard, Johnny? Where is my humble-hearted, best friend I once knew in school?" Johnny had to be reminded that kindness, compassion and forgiveness are not signs of being weak. He had to relearn, like far too many of us, that kindness, compassion, and forgiveness are signs of a humble, yet strong heart.

Paul was more concerned with the Christian heart than he was with the Christian head. Humble Christians possess tender hearts. When we as Christians refuse to acknowledge we have a hard heart, we are pleading our own case, not the case of Christ, to this sinful and pagan culture. Genuine humility, kindness, compassion and forgiveness are matters of the heart and not the head, of strength and not weakness.

LIFE PRINCIPLE ⚒

Today's Life Principle: *The Christian Heart.* How do we apply this Life Principle on Day 23? It is by recognizing the **"Nine Abundant Fruit Found in the Christian Heart"**:

1. *Love:* There are four kinds of love expressed in the Greek New Testament. Divine, Friendship, Procreative and Family Love. Divine love is the highest type of love one might express. Friendship love is communal in nature and denotes brotherly love or kindness. Procreative love is expressed in marriage. Family love goes beyond the Christian family to a love for all of Mankind. The Bible says love is the most excellent way (1 Corinthians 12:31-13:13).

2. *Joy:* Joy is at the heart of every Christian. The measure of one's joy is predicated on the level of one's love for God.

3. *Peace:* Peace that remains is directly connected to joy. The richer the joy, is the deeper the peace.

4. *Longsuffering:* Longsuffering or patient determination is the abundant fruit of personal refinement. Longsuffering enriches joy, deepens peace, strengthens love and produces perseverance.

5. *Kindness:* Kindness is closely related to the fruits of goodness, faithfulness, gentleness and self-control. All are expressions of what is visible to the human eye.

6. *Goodness:* Goodness is the fruit of godly character. Character is who we are when we are not on display.

7. *Faithfulness:* Faithfulness is the fruit of persistent faith. Without faith, it is impossible to please God (Hebrews 11:6).

8. *Gentleness:* Gentleness is the fruit of relational warmth and the mark of genuine humility.

9. *Self-control:* Self-control is the fruit of restraint. Restraint is not holding back, but being held by God's Holy Spirit.

Do you possess a fruitful Christian heart? Is your heart filled with the fruit of the Spirit of God? If not…then…repent.

LIFE JOURNEY

Personal Life Reflection: What did God say to you today?

_____

_____

_____

_____

_____

_____

_____

The New Journey Prayer using A.C.T.S. (Adoration, Confession, Thanksgiving and Supplication – page 19-20}:

1. Pray and ask your Heavenly Father to strengthen you and develop each of the "Nine Abundant Fruits Found in the Christian Heart."
2. Anger squelches while love liberates Christian compassion. Take a few minutes and examine your anger/compassion ratio. Pray that your righteous fruit will minister to the hearts of Man. See pages 246-248.
3. Ask God to fill our churches with Christian compassion and genuine love.

Fast: Abstain from eating one meal.

DAY 24

FOCUS: GOD

Time: _____

Date: _____

Daily Goal:

_____

_____

_____

_____

_____

_____

_____

_____

_____

Live Agapé

"The rebellious slogan 'All for love' is really love's death warrant (date of execution, for the moment, left blank)."

– C. S. Lewis,
The Four Loves,
pp. 166-167

LIFE STORY

Our Goal is to Imitate Jesus Christ to Live Agapé
Read and Meditate: Ephesians 5:2

"And walk in love, as the Messiah also loved us and gave Himself for us, a sacrificial and fragrant offering to God" (Eph. 5:2, HCSB).

Mary and Brian joyfully celebrated their Silver Anniversary. Brian was a man of few words. He was taught that if your words lacked visible action, you should refrain from engaging in verbose and elaborate conversations to convey truth.

Agapé love is not about meaningless dialogue and prideful monologue. Agapé love is to be demonstrated in one's daily life. Christians are charged according to the Scriptures to "walk it before you talk it." True religion is lifestyle driven. Paul says, *"...as the Messiah also loved us and gave Himself for us..."* Authentic agapé love always craves ways to express itself. These expressions of agapé love are never made with a begrudging spirit, but from an authentic heart. Agapé love is expressed as an aromatic sacrifice, experienced in the nature and person of the Lord Jesus Christ.

Live agapé! Convey a message of love in action. Christian love in action is agapé love in human form. Christ provided us with this kind of love in High Definition (HD). It is unconditional love despite its Adamic roots (Genesis 3). Brian's love for Mary illustrated human love in action. In the same way, Christians should imitate Christ and make living agapé God's standard. Why then are we as Christians failing to walk in agapé love each day?

LIFE PRINCIPLE ✕

Today's Life Principle: *Agapé.* Our Life Story is about learning to imitate the agapé love of Christ. How do we apply this Life Principle on Day 24? By learning and practicing the **"Four Demonstrations of Living Agapé"** which are:

1. *Agapé Gentleness:* Gentleness is a matter of personal choice. God has granted us the free will to demonstrate to the world that He did not create extraterrestrial, fallen beings cloaked in human flesh. We are ordinary people commissioned by God to achieve extraordinary things. Demonstrating agapé gentleness is gentleness beyond human ability and it demands divine participation. God's love is expressed through gentleness. We become the vehicles through which God conveys His profound Hesed Love (i.e., Old Testament expression of love meaning loving-kindness).

2. *Agapé Compassion:* Compassion is directly from the heart of our Heavenly Father. Our hearts are synchronized with His heart and we submit to being employed by Him.

3. *Agapé Understanding:* Human understanding is one thing, but agapé understanding is altogether different. Agapé understanding is at a deeper level because we understand the heart of others through the heart of God.

4. *Agapé Obedience:* To obey our parents is precious and powerful. To obey a dictator is a matter of life and death. To obey God is agapé obedience. This obedience is being clay surrendered into the loving hands of the Master Potter.

LIFE JOURNEY

Personal Life Reflection: What did God say to you today?

_____

_____

_____

_____

_____

_____

_____

The New Journey Prayer using A.C.T.S. (Adoration, Confession, Thanksgiving and Supplication – page 19-20):

1. After spending time in prayer and sharing with your pastor and/or leadership, determine to start a PrayerDiscipleship™ Group in your church. Make the agapé love of Jesus the primary focus in your PrayerDiscipleship™ small group. Refer to page 186.
2. Pray for the next seven days that there will be the spirit of agapé love infusing your heart and the heart of your church family throughout this year and beyond.
3. Pray for the next generation of leaders.

Fast: Abstain from eating one meal.

DAY 25

FOCUS: GOD

Time: _____

Date: _____

Daily Goal:

_____

_____

_____

_____

_____

_____

_____

_____

_____

_____

House Cleaning Time

"Hatred has its pleasures. It is therefore often the compensation by which a frightened man reimburses himself for the miseries of Fear. The more he fears, the more he will hate."

– C. S. Lewis,
The Screwtape Letters, p. 136

LIFE STORY

It's House Cleaning Time: Clean Up Your Hearts
Read and Meditate: Ephesians 5:3-6

"But sexual immorality and any impurity or greed should not even be heard of among you, as is proper for saints. Coarse and foolish talking or crude joking are not suitable, but rather giving thanks. For know and recognize this: Every sexually immoral or impure or greedy person, who is an idolater, does not have an inheritance in the kingdom of the Messiah and of God" (Eph. 5:3-6, HCSB).

King David disappointed the Lord God Almighty. He engaged in sexual immorality. His motives were often impure. His heart was contaminated with greed. Yet the Lord God Almighty chose not to disinherit him. God often referred to him as a man after His own heart. What set David apart from his contemporaries?

David passionately sought God's forgiveness. The king of Israel chose to repent of his sins to the King of Creation. In Psalm 51:3-4 (NLV), one of David's premiere repentant Psalms, he said, *"For I know my wrong doing, and my sin is always in front of me. I have sinned against You, and You only. I have done what is sinful in Your eyes."* [1] King David sought the mercy of God and God's mercy restored him.

God wants to do the very same for you and me. Like David, God invites each of us to engage in spiritual house cleaning. Genuine repentance is our soap and godly restoration is our reward. The question is, do we think God forgives premeditated acts of sin or do we think He plays by the rule, "One strike and you are out?"

---

[1] Psalm 51, "David's Confession of Sin," *New Life Version (NLV)*, 1969.

LIFE PRINCIPLE ✕

Today's Life Principle: *Forgiveness.* How do we apply this Life Principle on Day 25? It is achieved when God opens the **"Final Door of Forgiveness"**.

What is that Final Door of Forgiveness? The Apostle Paul in his letter to one of the most gifted churches in all of Asia Minor defines this final door of forgiveness in 1 Corinthians 13:1-13 as "charity" or "love." Paul writes, *"Though I speak with the tongues of men and of angels, and have not charity (love), I am become as sounding brass, or a tinkling cymbal"* (vs. 1).

There appears to be a conflict between the tongue and one's action. Speaking right words are often encouraging and influencing. However, if these words are absent of action, then they are simply words spoken amiss. God's words are words of substance and truth.

God loved King David. David lost his way, but God refused to lose or lessen His love for David. When a man or woman commits a grievous sin, God's charity or love covers the brokenness caused by our sin. When David acknowledged his ghastly sin and repented, God proceeded to open the final door of forgiveness.

Imagine eavesdropping on God's private conversation with the repentant, ashamed and broken king of Israel. Based on 1 Cor. 13, God most likely said, "David, my charity (agapé love) suffers long for you. It is kind, not envious. It is not boastful or puffed up. It does not behave disrespectfully or seek its own. It is not easily provoked and thinks no evil. It rejoices not in iniquity, but rejoices in the truth. It bears all things, believes all things, hopes all things and endures all things. "My love for you, David, will never fail, even when you fail Me."

LIFE JOURNEY

Personal Life Reflection: What did God say to you today?

_____

_____

_____

_____

_____

_____

_____

The New Journey Prayer using A.C.T.S. (Adoration, Confession, Thanksgiving and Supplication – page 19-20):

1. Pray that every room in the house of your heart has been scrubbed clean by God.
2. Be in agreement with God by being in the presence of God as often as possible.
3. Agreement with God begins and ends with a clean heart. Is your heart clean?
4. Look at "The Seven Dynamic Purposes for Fasting and Praying". Refer to page 204 and ask God what He would have you do.

Fast: Abstain from eating one meal.

DAY 26

FOCUS: GOD

Time: _____

Date: _____

Daily Goal:

_____

_____

_____

_____

_____

_____

_____

_____

_____

_____

A Life Change

"What you see and hear depends a good deal on where you are standing: it also depends on what sort of person you are."

– C. S. Lewis,
*The Magician's
Nephew*, p. 125

LIFE STORY

There has been a Change in My Life

Read and Meditate: Ephesians 5:8-10

"For ye were sometimes darkness, but now are ye light in the Lord: walk as children of light: (For the fruit of the Spirit is in all goodness and righteousness and truth;) Proving what is acceptable unto the Lord" (Eph. 5:8-10).

"Sometimes I am my own worst enemy," Monica mumbled. Monica had only been a Christian for six months. She had given up several shallow relationships and habits that had plagued her for many years. Yet in recent days, Monica felt as if she was her own worst enemy.

Paul wanted the Believers in the province of Ephesus to recognize salvation did not entail human perfection. He knew there would be periods when even the most committed journey traveler would feel the weight and pressure of long-forgotten sins. When God forgives sin, it is utterly forgiven. Pardon of sin involves God's vindication of the sin once held against us. *"So if the Son sets you free, you will be free indeed"*(John 8:36, NIV). *"If God is for us, who can be against us"* (Romans 8:31b, NIV).

Monica eventually learned when God forgives sin, it is utterly forgiven. Monica's life changed because she understood she had received God's full pardon. Monica's life is not the only life changed by the Lord Jesus Christ. All of us were once in darkness, but now we are in the Light of our Lord Jesus Christ. When Jesus changes a life, He lights a lamp within our soul that never darkens or fades away. He is our Eternal Light, the Lamp which lights a changed life. Can the Light of God force any of us to come out of our darkness?

LIFE PRINCIPLE ✕

Today's Life Principle: *Light.* How do we apply this Life Principle on Day 26? Through realizing the Light of God will not force us to come out is of our darkness. There are **"Four Things the Light of God Refuses to Force Us to Do"**:

1. *Confess our sins:* Confession of sin is when we agree with God's assessment of us. We say to God, "God you are right. I have sinned and fallen short of Your glory." That's confession of sin. God never forces us to confess our sins.

2. *Repent of our sins:* Repentance of sin is not the same as confession of sin. Repentance of sin occurs when we decide to change the way we've been living. It is a 180-degree turn in the opposite direction. Repenting is our choice.

3. *Obey God's Word:* Obedience is more than doing a lot of nifty things to impress God and Man. God does not long for what we can do to make Him or ourselves look good. God simply calls us to obey. It's up to us to decide how we'll respond.

4. *Enter Heaven to live with God forever:* If we don't want to go to Heaven, God will not place a gun in our back and force us. If we really prefer Hell over Heaven, God will allow us to make our bed in the Lake of Fire. God refuses to force His will on us. Free will belongs to us. Going to Hell or Heaven is solely our decision to make.

LIFE JOURNEY

Personal Life Reflection: What did God say to you today?

_____

_____

_____

_____

_____

_____

_____

_____

The New Journey Prayer using A.C.T.S. (Adoration, Confession, Thanksgiving and Supplication – page 19-20):

1. Pray for Christians all over the world that we will walk in the Light of the Lord.
2. Pray for God to send revival and spiritual awakening.
3. Pray for America.
4. Believe with all your heart wherever there is God's Light, darkness flees. Begin today to walk in the Light of the Lord daily.

Fast: **Abstain from eating two meals, viewing television for 24 hours and attending secular movies.**

DAY 27

FOCUS: GOD

Time: _____

Date: _____

Daily Goal:

_____

_____

_____

_____

_____

_____

_____

_____

_____

Lord, Help!!!

"You've seen your Godzilla. The question is: is he all you see?"

– Max Lucado,
Facing Your Giants, p. 4

LIFE STORY

Just Say No
Read and Meditate: Ephesians 5:11-14

"And have no fellowship with the unfruitful works of darkness, but rather reprove them" (Eph. 5:11).

"No means no, Robert." These were the razor sharp cutting words of my mom, Gladys Louise Loggins. Her philosophy was stern and straightforward. "Say what you mean and mean what you say." My mother believed one should never substitute an emphatic "no" with a probable "yes."

Just say "no." The Bible clearly says, *"And have no fellowship with the unfruitful works of darkness..."* Just say "no" to ungodliness and disobedience to the Lord Jesus Christ. Because ungodly behavior and unrighteous deeds produce the destructive works of darkness and death.

Saying "no" insulates us from the ways of the world. *The New Journey* is learning how to apply the wisdom in the Word of God to life on a daily basis. Never substitute a right for a wrong. Strive to live a righteous life and not simply engage in doing right things. Allow God's Word to make changes. Seek the wisdom of God's Word with an even deeper passion. Understand that academic intellectualism is not equivalent to biblical spiritualism. Life in the Spirit is about knowing God and living the Spirit-filled Christian life.

In the prophetic, wise words of my mama, "Just say no!" Learn to say "no" to the ways of the world, but "yes" to the work and wisdom of God. Genuine fellowship with Almighty God demands work and wisdom. Unfruitful – even deadly – words or deeds can be avoided when applying what my mama said. God's direction to say "no" is always better than Man's encouragement to say "yes."

LIFE PRINCIPLE

Today's Life Principle: *No.* How do we apply this Life Principle on Day 27? By being able to embrace God's "no" instead of Man's "yes" through **"Six Incontrovertible 'No's' of God"**:

1. *Academic Intellectualism:* Human intelligence is not a negative. God gave all mankind an ability to reason above all His other creations. There is nothing wrong with a man using his mind to achieve great things. God will say "no" to those who depend more on our minds than on our Master. Our Master must never take a back seat to our minds. Whenever our mind attempts to take control, just say "no." God's "no" is never a "yes".

2. *Super Spiritualism:* God is not impressed with super spiritualism. Doing super spiritual things never outweighs being Spirit-filled (Eph. 5:18). God wants us to say "no" to super spirituality because it only leads to religious pride. The proud will fall prostrate to God's "no".

3. *Disobedience:* God has commanded we make disciples (Matthew 28:18-20). When it comes to being disobedient to God's call to be disciplers, the answer is "no".

4. *Unfruitfulness:* Don't ever say "yes" if God has already said "no". When God says "no", immediately agree with Him and proceed to your new assignment. If we are to produce fruit, God's "no" never means "yes". It is unwholesome and will never lead to wholeness.

5. *Ungodliness:* *"Do not let any unwholesome talk come out of your mouth"* (Eph. 4:29a NIV). Say "no" to anything that is not said for the glory of God.

6. *Death:* God looked spiritual death directly in the eye and said, "no". The Bible says, *"The last enemy to be destroyed is death"* (1 Cor. 15:26) and *"Death has been swallowed up in victory"* (1 Cor. 15:54b). Death was rendered powerless at Calvary because God said, "no" to death. We must say "no" to spiritually dead things to live in the victory of God over death.

Personal Life Reflection: What did God say to you today?

_____

_____

_____

_____

_____

_____

_____

The New Journey Prayer using A.C.T.S. (Adoration, Confession, Thanksgiving and Supplication – page 19-20):

1. When confronted by peer pressure, pray our children know how to say "no".
2. Say "yes" to God before He questions you today.
3. Decide you will not engage in ungodly ways or have fellowship with the wicked and fallen world.
4. How many persons are on your prayer list? Why not ask God to show you one person He wants added to your list?

Fast: **Abstain from eating one meal and refrain from listening to secular media.**

DAY 28

FOCUS: GOD

Time: _____

Date: _____

Daily Goal:

_____

_____

_____

_____

_____

_____

_____

_____

_____

Living Wise

"Those who wish to succeed must ask the right preliminary questions."

– *Aristotle,*
Metaphysics, II, (III), I,
C. S. Lewis,
The Complete C.S.
Lewis Signature
Classics, p. 303

LIFE STORY

Wise Living
Read and Meditate: Ephesians 5:15-16

"See then that ye walk circumspectly, not as fools, but as wise, Redeeming the time, because the days are evil" (Eph. 5:15-16). *"Where is the wise? where is the scribe? where is the disputer of this world? hath not God made foolish the wisdom of this world?"* (1 Corinthians 1:20).

Three consecutive times Paul the Apostle asks "Where? – Where is the wise? Where is the scribe? Where is the disputer?..." Paul's questions are not asked in ignorance, but are posed to stimulate the hearer's mind. He wants God's people to stop and think and take an introspective examination of their immediate environment. Wisdom takes time. Wise living is a lifelong process. Becoming a person of wisdom doesn't happen overnight. Learning to live wisely is costly.

Notice Paul's first word in verse 15, *"See..."*. What does Paul encourage Believers to see? He wants all of us to see what is visible through the Spirit's eye, not what is visible through the physical eye. Relying on our physical sight produces foolish results. When God's timing is ignored, our walk often strays from the path of righteousness. Godly, spiritual sight enables us to *"...walk circumspectly"* – purposefully, with dignity and no distraction. This leads to redeeming the time God has provided for us to achieve God's purpose in our life. Why is this so critical? Because the days are evil and we must redeem the time. James the Elder is in full agreement with the Apostle Paul. Was deeply concerned about redeeming the time and living wisely. Are you careful how you live your life and redeem your time? Are you living your life wisely? Is there any such thing as a winning walk of wisdom?

LIFE PRINCIPLE

Today's Life Principle: *Wisdom.* How do we apply this Life Principle on Day 28? By developing **"The Winning Walk of Wisdom"**:

1. ***Walk Carefully***: Foolish people congregate together like a flock of thoughtless birds vulnerable to any passing hunter. Walking with foolish people often leads those who could be wise to become foolish. *"Do not answer a fool according to his folly, or you will be like him yourself"* (Proverbs 26:4). Walk with fools and we will soon become the same role model as our companions.

2. ***Walk Faithfully:*** Abraham was a man of great faith. He was referred to as the "Father of the Faithful" in Hebrews 11, the "Faith" chapter. *"...without faith it is impossible to please God"* (Hebrews 11:6, NIV). So pleasing God is directly proportionate to our walking in the realm of faith.

3. ***Walk Courageously or Fearlessly:*** Fear has no place for those who endeavor to launch out on the winning walk of wisdom. *"The fear of the Lord is the beginning of wisdom..."* (Prov. 9:10a)." One of the best ways to walk fearlessly is to tap into the wellspring of the wisdom of God through Biblical fear.

4. ***Walk Firmly:*** We need to establish a firm walk. God challenged Joshua to walk firmly when He said *"I will give you every place where you set your foot"* (Josuah 1:3a, NIV). The winning walk of wisdom is a firm walk of faith and obedience.

LIFE JOURNEY

Personal Life Reflection: What did God say to you today?

_____

_____

_____

_____

_____

_____

_____

The New Journey Prayer using A.C.T.S. (Adoration, Confession, Thanksgiving and Supplication – page 19-20):

1. Ask God to provide you with a "Firm Walk."

2. Pray for our political leaders to seek a daily walk in the ways of God.

3. Pray for wisdom in everything you do today.

Fast: Abstain from eating one meal and refrain from listening to secular media.

DAY 29

FOCUS: GOD

Time: _____

Date: _____

Daily Goal:

_____

_____

_____

_____

_____

_____

_____

_____

_____

_____

Moving From...To

"Christianity helps us face the music, even when we don't like the tune."

– E. C. McKenzie, *Quips & Quotes,* p. 173

LIFE STORY

Spirit Filled Living
Read and Meditate: Ephesians 5:17-18

"Wherefore be ye not unwise, but understanding what the will of the Lord is. And be not drunk with wine, wherein is excess; but be filled with the Spirit," (Eph. 5:17-18).

Moses Nguyễn was a Spirit-filled, senior pastor in a small village in South Vietnam. God used his life greatly. Pastor Nguyễn said, "I pray, then walk and pray again as I travel from place to place." He saw himself as traveling on a journey to help his fellow man to receive Jesus Christ as personal Lord and Savior.

Spirit-filled living begins with one decision: to be filled with the Spirit. Paul never says, "Engage in Spirit-filled activities or events." Rather, *"...be filled with the Spirit of God."* (v. 18) There is a profound difference in doing church work versus doing the work of the church. Church work often consumes the life of far too many church members. They never legitimately step on the path of *The New Journey*. Being busy is no substitute for living the Spirit-filled life. It is about understanding, embracing and applying God's will. A Spirit-filled saint is one who seeks to be "drunk" in the Spirit of God, leading to authenticity and righteousness.

Pastor Moses Nguyễn agreed with the Apostle Paul about being filled with the Spirit of the Living God. When God fills a saint with the Holy Spirit, he or she will learn the satisfaction of being filled daily. The mark of foolishness is operating in the flesh. Spirit-filled Christians operate through the Holy Spirit. Are you a Spirit-filled Christian?

LIFE PRINCIPLE

Today's Life Principle: *The Spirit Filled Life.* How do we apply this Life Principle on Day 29? By learning the **"Four Characteristics of an Authentic, Spirit-filled Life"**:

1. *Complete Humility:* Humility is incomplete without the inner working power of the Holy Spirit of God. The Holy Spirit is our Divine Counselor who helps us hear God's voice more clearly and effectively. Understanding God's language requires a Spirit connection to the One who surrendered up His Spirit at the time of His crucifixion. "It is finished then he surrendered up the Holy Spirit" (John 19:30). Jesus did not say, *"He was finished,"* but *"It is finished."* He had finished His assignment. His humility at the cross becomes our humility at His resurrection. Complete humility requires total surrender.

2. *Profound Patience:* The old adage says, "Patience is a virtue." Profound patience is found in one who has willingly accepted the Spirit-filled life as Christ modeled it for all New Testament Believers. We are charged by God to administer patience to one another. As we learn to wait upon the Lord and receive renewed strength, we are to equally practice profound patience and wait upon one another to develop His inner bond. That bond comes only through the pneuma (i.e., Spirit) of God.

3. *Pure Love:* Pure love is distilled and filtered through the blood of Jesus. Pure love has been sanctified by His death and resurrected by His grace and mercy. Our challenge as Spirit-filled believers is to practice the love Jesus preached.

4. *Imitative Submission:* Imitative submission intertwines two concepts into one compelling insight. As Spirit-filled believers, we are called to walk in wisdom and submit to the Person of Christ. Imitative submission reflects agreement with the oneness embedded in the Trinity. It is our submission to the will of God.

LIFE JOURNEY

Personal Life Reflection: What did God say to you today?

_____

_____

_____

_____

_____

_____

The New Journey Prayer using A.C.T.S. (Adoration, Confession, Thanksgiving and Supplication – page 19-20):

1. Seek to be a Spirit-filled Christian.
2. Believe God when it comes to the supernatural work of the Holy Spirit of God in your life.
3. Ask God to fill each of your church's leaders with the Holy Spirit daily.
4. Have you won any victories as a result of being persistent in prayer?
5. How many days have you surrendered to the Lord in both prayer and fasting?

Fast: **Abstain from eating one meal and refrain from listening to secular media.**

DAY 30

FOCUS: GOD

Time: _____

Date: _____

Daily Goal:

_____

_____

_____

_____

_____

_____

_____

_____

_____

The Language of Love & Peace

The Great Sin:
"For Pride is spiritual cancer: it eats up the very possibility of love, or contentment, or even common sense."

– C. S. Lewis,
Mere Christianity,
p. 97

LIFE STORY

Learning How to Speak Peace
Read and Meditate: Ephesians 5:19-20

"...speaking to one another in psalms, hymns and spiritual songs, singing and making music to the Lord in your heart..." (Eph. 5:19-20, HCSB).

Doris Chung was the Senior Vice President of a Fortune 500, worldwide communication and technology company in New York. Doris was soft spoken in meetings that were often volatile and hostile. Her countenance was enveloped by a tranquil spirit of peace. Although Doris Chung was small in stature and gentle in demeanor, her words of peace pierced the soul with simple truth, personal compassion and persuasive power.

Speaking peace is not simply about articulating soft words to impress others. Doris Chung was fully aware of the power she wielded in her corporation. More importantly, she enjoyed a vibrant relationship with John, the company's owner and Chief Executive Officer (CEO). John trusted Doris's wisdom. She had proven her loyalty to him and to the mission of his company. For 20 years Doris was a stabilizing force in a company on the cusp of explosive worldwide growth.

As we travel on *The New Journey*, our Heavenly Father, our "Eternal CEO," has given us an assignment to bring others to wholeness and holiness in Christ. This will never happen unless we are whole and holy ourselves. One of the signs of spiritual wholeness and holiness is inner peace. *The New Journey* travelers must possess inner peace to speak peace. Outer peace will never materialize until there is an inner peace. May we seek inner peace and speak peace into the lives of others. Do you know how to speak peace and talk Christian?

LIFE PRINCIPLE

Today's Life Principle: *Christian Talk.* How do we apply this Life Principle on Day 30? By learning to fluently speak the **"Spirit-filled Christian Language"** and avoid speaking like any of the following:

1. *Sam Slander:* Sam Slander speaks badly of others and damages reputations. He's should be marked absent.

2. *Gloria Gossip:* Gloria has been hiding behind sharing "prayer requests" for years. She creates such profound disharmony, until the entire leadership team has to pray and fast.

3. *Bill Bitterness:* Bill apparently was born with a bitter tongue. He needs to lighten up and sweeten up.

4. *Larry Liar:* Larry can lie his way out of almost anything. He is a highly believable liar, but is rarely dependable.

5. *David Deceiver:* David seems to exemplify the character of the real King David, but he deceives others while acting as if they are his closest companions. David is not genuine or trustworthy.

6. *Francis Un-Forgiveness:* Francis does not practice the power of a forgiving heart. Forgiveness is not her strength. Francis would rather hold a grudge.

7. *Roger Rudeness:* Roger learned how to be rude from his dad. His father was the epitome of rudeness and one of the most ill-mannered men in the city. Roger remains a cold-blooded, rude community leader.

8. *Helen Hopelessness:* Helen became a hopeless person several years ago and she refuses to change her hopeless ways. She sees no hope in change.

9. *Paula Pride:* Paula was Helen's best friend. Due to her pride, she didn't help Helen and also refuses to change.

LIFE JOURNEY

Personal Life Reflection: What did God say to you today?

_____

_____

_____

_____

_____

_____

_____

The New Journey Prayer using A.C.T.S. (Adoration, Confession, Thanksgiving and Supplication – page 19-20):

1. Have you ever met one of the people listed on page 139?
2. Have you ever been one yourself?
3. Refer to pages 253-255 and read the Scripture dealing with controlling the tongue.
4. Pray we as Christians improve how we use our tongues to be proper witnesses to those who have not received Jesus Christ as Savior and Lord.

Fast: Abstain from eating one meal and refrain from listening to secular media.

DAY 31

FOCUS: GOD

Time: _____

Date: _____

Daily Goal:

_____

_____

_____

_____

_____

_____

_____

_____

_____

_____

Biblical Submission

The Great Sin:
"If you think you are
not conceited, it
means you are very
conceited indeed."

– C. S. Lewis,
Mere Christianity,
p. 99

 # LIFE STORY

The Submitting Family
Part 1: Biblical Submission
Read and Meditate: Ephesians 5:21

"...submitting to one another in the fear of Christ" (Eph. 5:21, HCSB).

In the "good old days," I was taught to fear (i.e., reverence or respect) those in authority. I vividly remember storming into the house following my second week of school and complaining to my mom and big brother about how Miss Scott, my sixth grade teacher, corrected me in front of my peers. While I was telling my story, my big brother quietly slipped into the kitchen to eat dinner. My mom continued listening carefully and prayerfully to me as I accused my teacher of embarrassing me and disrespecting my feelings. Without notice, my mom said, "Robert, step outside and fetch me a switch (branch) from the peach tree so I can teach you how to appreciate correction and discipline." On that day, I came to understand the biblical relationship between submission and fear.

Biblical submission most often begins with a clear understanding of fear/respect. To fear God does not mean to hate God. You can learn to fear God and love Him simultaneously. Peace, love, joy, compassion and genuine submission are birthed out of biblical respect.

Biblical submission knows no gender. Adam and Eve submitted to one another as they submitted to God. The word for biblical submission is "hupotasso." Hupotasso is Greek for expressing a military idea, "to rank under." But remember, biblical submission always emanates from a godly fear or respect. Should we as Christians mix fear with submission?

LIFE PRINCIPLE

Today's Life Principle: *Fearful Submission.* How do we apply this Life Principle on Day 31? By understanding the **"Three Christian Expressions of Fearful Submission"**:

1. ***"Yes, Lord":*** The word "Lord" might be better expressed as Master, Teacher, or Rabbi. Inherent in this expression is the biblical idea of student and teacher. Fearful submission requires an object and an objective. The object is the student, the objective is the pursuant goal of the Master. "Yes, Lord" is not crafted in an interrogative. This is not a question. Fearful submission does not ask questions, it provides declarative statements. The Lord speaks and we are compelled to respond. However, our individual and corporate responses are always a matter of choice.

2. ***"I am Yours, Lord":*** The word "am" is from the root word "to be." The student says to the Master Teacher, "I am Yours to do with as You please. I do not have ownership over my life. Lord, my life is in Your hands. You are my Teacher and Coach. I am incapable of doing anything on my own. I need You to guide me into the realm of fearful submission."

3. ***"I will obey":*** This is the final expression of one who has genuinely embraced fearful submission. It has been said that "Life begins at 40, 50, 60..." I would suggest life that possesses God's supernatural blessing and benefits begins at the point of submission. Are you a fearfully submitted Christian? If not, why?

LIFE JOURNEY

Personal Life Reflection: What did God say to you today?

_____

_____

_____

_____

_____

_____

_____

The New Journey Prayer using A.C.T.S. (Adoration, Confession, Thanksgiving and Supplication – page 19-20):

1. Are you and your family fearfully submitted to God?
2. Pray you and your family will experience the joy of submission.
3. Ask the Lord Jesus Christ to teach you and your family the joy of submission as a lifestyle.
4. Is your family with you on *The New Journey*? Are you as a family keeping a family and friends prayer list (pages 259-260)?

Fast: **Abstain from eating one meal and refrain from listening to secular media.**

DAY 32

FOCUS: GOD

Time: _____

Date: _____

Daily Goal:

_____

_____

_____

_____

_____

_____

_____

_____

_____

_____

The Submitting Wife

The Great Sin:
"The utmost evil is Pride. Unchastity, anger, greed, drunkenness, and all that, are mere fleabites in comparison: it was through Pride that the devil became the devil: Pride leads to every other vice: it is the complete anti-God state of mind."

– C. S. Lewis,
Mere Christianity,
p. 94

LIFE STORY

The Submitting Family
Part 2: Wives
Read and Meditate: Ephesians 5:22-24

"Wives, submit to your own husbands as to the Lord, for the husband is the head of the wife as Christ is the head of the church. He is the Savior of the body. Now as the church submits to Christ, so wives are to submit to their husbands in everything" (Eph. 5:22-24, HCSB).

Several years ago, one of my beloved church members wanted to purchase a beautiful, name-brand suit for me. I asked her if she had shared with her husband her gracious offer. "No, I haven't," she said. "Pastor, why is it necessary for me to do this? This money is my money. Pastor, I'm my own person."

Sally failed to realize what the Scripture says about honoring and respecting her husband. Her unwillingness to submit to Christ first created problems with her ability to submit to her husband. Christ is the Head of the Church. The husband is the head of the wife.

I refused to accept Sally's kind, yet unbiblical gesture. She meant well, but she failed to obey the principle of submission in God's Word. Submission is not about power, it's about a Person – Jesus. The beginning of a successful marriage is godly submission.

Proper biblical order in marital relationships always demands obedience to headship. Is your relationship with your husband out of order? Do you need order in your marital relationship? If you do, repent, submit to God and turn to Him immediately (2 Chronicles 7:14). What steps will you take to strengthen your marriage through Godly submission?

LIFE PRINCIPLE ✕

Today's Life Principle: *Submissive Wives.* How do we apply this Life Principle on Day 32? By learning how to extinguish the **"Four Beginnings of a Bad Marriage"**:

1. ***Extinguish All Disrespect:*** A disrespectful wife is an irritant to her husband. Most, if not all, husbands do not want to be treated like a child. Even though too many husbands are still playing basketball and video games with their peers at age 50, they want and need your respect. The best place to start is with prayer. You will find God truly answers prayer. Place your husband on the altar of the Lord and leave him there for God to do the finishing work in his life. Talk less and pray more. Give God time to upgrade your husband.

2. ***Extinguish Cancerous Division:*** Don't allow the cancerous spirit of division to infect your relationship with your husband. Practice immediate forgiveness in order to reap immediate rewards (Matthew 6:9-13).

3. ***Extinguish Unholy Disloyalty:*** Beware of treating other men with more respect than you do your husband. Doing this creates an unholy spirit of disloyalty and disfavor. Every husband needs a loyal wife, even when he does not act like he deserves one.

4. ***Extinguish All Satanic Deception:*** Don't allow the spirit of Satan to come between you and your husband like Eve did in Genesis 3. Practice being a submissive wife. Submission is really about you and God. Submit now.

LIFE JOURNEY

Personal Life Reflection: What did God say to you today?

_____

_____

_____

_____

_____

_____

_____

The New Journey Prayer using A.C.T.S. (Adoration, Confession, Thanksgiving and Supplication – page 19-20):

1. Are you a submissive wife to your husband?
2. Is submitting to your husband a joy or a job?
3. Pray the Lord God Almighty pours into your soul the joy of submission this day.
4. Make a genuine commitment as a woman of the Word to practice submission to your husband as a lifestyle.
5. Identify times when you failed to practice submission to your husband.

Fast: **Abstain from eating one meal, viewing television, and opening email for four hours. Practice absolute silence for four hours.**

DAY 33

FOCUS: GOD

Time: _____

Date: _____

Daily Goal:

_____

_____

_____

_____

_____

_____

_____

_____

The Submitting Husband

The Great Sin:
"As long as you are proud you cannot know God. A proud man is always looking down on things and people: and, of course, as long as you are looking down, you cannot see something that is above you."

– C. S. Lewis,
Mere Christianity,
p. 96

LIFE STORY

The Submitting Family
Part 3: Husbands

Read and Meditate: Ephesians 5:25-33

"*Husbands, love your wives, just as also Christ loved the church and gave Himself for her to make her holy, cleansing her with the washing of water by the word*" (Eph. 5:25-26, HCSB).

"Love my wife as Christ loved the church? I don't believe it is humanly possible for me to achieve this type of extraordinary love." Adam was absolutely right. Bob knew this love could only come from Christ, so he decided to take God at His word. He began to love Helena as Christ loved the Church and gave Himself for Her.

Bob desired to care for his wife until death parted them. As God would have it, Bob preceded her in death. On the day he died, Bob was faithfully serving Helena and demonstrating agapé love (i.e., divine love) in an exemplary way. Less than a year later, Helena was united with Bob in Heaven.

Agapé love is a human impossibility; but nothing is impossible with God (Luke 1:37). Christ sacrificed His life on the cross at Calvary for His Bride, the Church. Bob likewise served his wife sacrificially. Serving her was his greatest honor and a sacred hope. Knowing he would see her again in Glory came from the hope that never fails. How will you use Bob as a model and serve your wife?

LIFE PRINCIPLE ✕

Today's Life Principle: *Serving Husbands.* How do we apply this Life Principle on Day 33? By practicing the **"Four Historical Ministries for Healing Wounded Marriages"**:

1. ***Ministry of Encouragement:*** Be your wife's best cheerleader Cheer her on in the things she cherishes most. Build her up and esteem her more highly than you do yourself. She should be your top priority immediately after God (Matthew 6:33). Learn how to practice the ministry of encouragement to perfection. Set a goal each day to say or do something to encourage your bride.

2. ***Ministry of Example:*** Be a godly example of Christ. Christ loved the Church and gave Himself up willingly and joyfully. Step up your game. Be more and more like Christ (2 Corinthians 5:17).

3. ***Ministry of Service:*** My wife has the gift of hospitality. She loves to cook and entertain family, friends and members of our church. She is one of the best cooks on this planet. The ministry of service does not come natural for me. My wife has helped me improve my ministry of service over the past several years. She has been an excellent role model. Now, I have been knighted the master of the barbeque grill. Serving in the pulpit is wonderful, but at home the joy of serving in the barbeque pit is altogether different.

4. ***Ministry of Sacrifice:*** Read Galatians 2:20 and sacrifice your own desires for your wife.

LIFE JOURNEY

Personal Life Reflection: What did God say to you today?

_____

_____

_____

_____

_____

_____

_____

The New Journey Prayer using A.C.T.S. (Adoration, Confession, Thanksgiving and Supplication – page 19-20):

1. Do you genuinely love your wife as Christ loved and died for the Church?
2. Resolve to love her as Christ loved.
3. Pray you will demonstrate an exemplary model of marital love for your wife before your children. Be authentic and Spirit-filled.
4. Refer to pages 234-238 and read what the Bible teaches about holiness – "Be Holy!"
5. As a man of God, practice holiness and loving-kindness in your marital relationship.
6. Do you pray for your wife daily and do you have designated prayer times?

Fast: Abstain from food for 24 four hours and practice absolute silence for the same 24 four hours.

DAY 34

FOCUS: GOD

Time: _____

Date: _____

Daily Goal:

_____

_____

_____

_____

_____

_____

_____

_____

_____

Submitting Children

The Great Sin:
"The vain person wants praise, applause, admiration too much and is always angling for it."

– C. S. Lewis,
Mere Christianity,
p. 97

LIFE STORY

The Submitting Family
Part 4: Children
Read and Meditate: Ephesians 6:1-3

"Children, obey your parents as you would the Lord, because this is right. Honor your father and mother, which is the first commandment with a promise, so that it may go well with you and that you may have a long life in the land" (Eph. 6:1-3, HCSB).

Is there any such thing as right or wrong? In our culture today, right or wrong is determined by one's personal choice. This is what Buddy was taught from the day he entered kindergarten to the day he graduated with a degree in business and finance. Since he graduated with numerous honors, Buddy had offers from around the world, but he decided to work for his father in the family business. Buddy became an instant success in the business, but, in reality, he was a painful disappointment. Buddy continually disrespected his father in staff and board meetings. He also disrespected senior salesmen on a daily basis. He was a dishonorable son.

Children are admonished to obey parental authority. However, Buddy not only failed to honor his father on Earth, he equally failed to honor his Father in Heaven. *"Honor your father and mother, which is the first commandment with a promise"* (vs. 2). R. A. Torrey says, "Absolute surrender to God is the secret of blessedness and power." [6] This is so true – children must obey. Are you and your parents part of a winning team? Do you obey their authority?

---

[6]R. A. Torrey, *Power-Filled Living: How To Receive God's Best For Your Life* (New Kensington, PA: Whitaker House, 1998), p. 69.

LIFE PRINCIPLE ✖

Today's Life Principle: *Honorable Children.* How do we apply this Life Principle on Day 34? By learning the **"Four Keys of Appreciation for Worthy and Unworthy Parents"**:

1. *Key of Honor:* When we honor our parents, we honor God. There may be times when parents do not deserve honor. At times parents can be out of line with God by correcting their children while refusing to own up to their own sin. We may not appreciate being corrected by parents unwilling to be corrected by God first, but the Lord still teaches us to honor our parents. Learn to allow God to parent each of us. Love and honor our parents, even when we don't necessarily like what they do.

2. *Key of Respect:* Even disrespectful parents want respect. It seems counter-intuitive, but true. Practice respecting all parents and guardians. God will "*add to your days*" (Exodus 20:12).

3. *Key of Obedience:* Obedience is the sweetest key to the hearts of parents. When obeying our parents, we demonstrate obedience to our Heavenly Father.

4. *Key of Surrender:* If we surrender to our parents before we surrender to God, we have failed to truly surrender. Read Romans 12:1-2.

LIFE JOURNEY

Personal Life Reflection: What did God say to you today?

_____

_____

_____

_____

_____

_____

_____

The New Journey Prayer using A.C.T.S. (Adoration, Confession, Thanksgiving and Supplication – page 19-20):

1. Are you a submissive child?
2. Identify genuine ways you can honor your parents with dignity and respect.
3. Ask God to change your heart if you have refused to honor your parents in the past.
4. When it comes to respecting your parents, pray to God for a sincere heart of flesh to melt your stubborn heart of stone.
5. Do your parents have regular family devotions?

Fast: Abstain from eating one meal.

DAY 35

FOCUS: GOD

Time: _____

Date: _____

Daily Goal:

_____

_____

_____

_____

_____

_____

_____

_____

_____

_____

Submitting Fathers

The Great Sin:
"Pride always means enmity – it is enmity. And not only enmity between man and man, but enmity to God."

– C. S. Lewis,
Mere Christianity,
p. 96

LIFE STORY

The Submitting Family
Part 5: Fathers
Read and Meditate: Ephesians 6:4

"Fathers, don't stir up anger in your children, but bring them up in the training and instruction of the Lord" (Eph. 6:4, HCSB).

At six years of age, my father died. However, the spirit of fatherhood did not die in my life. My pastor, Reverend C. D. Thomas, and the deacons of the St. Mark Baptist Church would become surrogate fathers to my sisters and brothers. Although my father died when I was six years of age, the wisdom and teachings of my surrogate fathers never died.

I am the man I am today because of the wisdom of two women, Gloria Langley (my mother) and Minnie Hawthorn (my aunt). Their philosophy of fraternal family leadership embraced this insightful truth: *It takes a woman to birth a boy, but it takes a man to birth a man.*

I am the father I am today not simply because of the influence of men in my life. The impact of my Heavenly Father on my soul as He saved and reared me, helped me to become a father on Earth as He is my Father in Heaven. I have learned fraternal family leadership always obligates me to lead by example. I must submit to my Heavenly Father before I can require submission from my family.

Biblical submission commands authority without demanding authority. *"Fathers, don't stir up anger in your children, but bring them up in the training and instruction of the Lord."* A man will never experience the joy of birthing a submitting son until he has become a submitted father. Are you a submitted son to your Heavenly Father?

LIFE PRINCIPLE

Today's Life Principle: *Submitted Fathers.* How do we apply this Life Principle on Day 35? By **"Polishing the Four Gems in the Life of Every Child"**:

1. *Gem of Courage:* No child comes into this world with an owner's manual, but if we are godly fathers, we have God's manual – the Bible – at our fingertips. God's holy and sacred Word teaches fathers to bestow needed courage upon their children. Who else besides a godly father can polish the gem of courage within them. Courage enables children to know how to stand when their friends are challenging them to bow down to the spirit of this Age – the spirit of ungodliness. God told Joshua to be a man of courage. When was the last time you actually encouraged your child? Polish the gem of courage within your son or daughter. Let them know how precious they are to you as their father on earth. Represent your Heavenly Father to your children the same way He represents Himself as a Father to you (Matthew 6).

2. *Gem of Compassion:* Far too many children have been crushed by this heartless, pagan culture. Be intentional. Practice polishing the gem of compassion by demonstrating your fatherly love in action. Compassion is never out of season for a child. The more the merrier.

3. *Gem of Commitment:* Fathers must first be committed to Christ before they can boldly disciple their children to become committed, mature adults. A father's modeling commitment is what every child needs.

4. *Gem of Christ-Likeness:* Read 2 Corinthians 5:17 and apply it today. Conclude with this question, "Which gem do I need to polish today?"

LIFE JOURNEY

Personal Life Reflection: What did God say to you today?

_____

_____

_____

_____

_____

_____

_____

_____

The New Journey Prayer using A.C.T.S. (Adoration, Confession, Thanksgiving and Supplication – page 19-20):

1. Strive to model the person of Christ to your children throughout all the stages of their lives.
2. Elevate your daughters as young Christian ladies and develop your sons as mighty men of God.
3. Pray God helps you control your temper with your children as the Spirit of God extinguishes your anger and/or rage. Refer again to pages 246-248, **"The 13 Tools for Dealing with Anger."**
4. Ask God to teach you the masterful skills of operating in the craft of fatherhood.
5. Do you have a personal prayer list with all your kids' names on it? Are you consistently praying for your kids?

Fast: **Abstain from eating one meal and refrain from all types of media.**

DAY 36

FOCUS: GOD

Time: _____

Date: _____

Daily Goal:

_____

_____

_____

_____

_____

_____

_____

_____

_____

Submitting Workers

The Great Sin:
"The real test of being in the presence of God is that you either forget about yourself altogether or see yourself as a small, dirty object. It is better to forget about yourself altogether."

– C. S. Lewis,
Mere Christianity,
p. 96-97

The Submitting Family
Part 6: Employees/Employers
Read and Meditate: Ephesians 6:5-9

"Slaves, obey your human masters with fear and trembling, in the sincerity of your heart, as to Christ... Serve with a good attitude, as to the Lord and not to men..." (Eph. 6:5, 7 HCSB).

Donald was totally confused as a new Christian following the pastor's Bible message on "Slaves for Christ." From studying American history, Donald remembered one of the greatest shames woven into the fabric and foundation of our nation's heritage was slavery. He saw slavery as one of the deepest scars on the face of our nation. Yet the Scripture appeared to teach slavery as not only an acceptable cultural allowance, but equally as an ultimate spiritual lifestyle of discipline. He thought to himself, "Does the Scripture contradict itself when it comes to propagating slavery in these manners? Should slavery be allowed today? Were the Founding Fathers of our nation correct when they allowed slavery to exist as a cultural norm and an economical necessity?"

After carefully examining the Scriptures, Donald finally understood his pastor's message. Using the word "slave" in the Apostle Paul's writings, God is inviting each of us to seek a deeply committed and disciplined life. God calls us to be slaves for Christ. *"Doulos"* is the Greek word for "bond slave." It relates to someone who is surrendered to an Earthly master. In the same way, as Christians, we are to surrender to our Heavenly Master. To be a slave for Christ is radical. A legitimate Journey traveler must become a slave. Submission is not a maybe, but a mandate.

LIFE PRINCIPLE ✕

Today's Life Principle: *Submissive Servants.* How do we apply this Life Principle on Day 36? By practicing the **"Four Non-Negotiable Attributes of a Faithful Servant Despite Having a Difficult Boss"**:

1. ***Positive Attitude:*** A positive attitude purifies a contaminated and ungodly atmosphere. Practice makes perfect. Perfecting the right kind of attitude is an illustration of a mature Christian (Eph. 4:14-16). Scripture says, *"Your attitude should be the same as that of Jesus Christ"* (Phillippians 2:5, NIV). Godly servants possess the power to change the climate created by an ungodly boss. Disputes and bickering with your boss are not the solution. Learn how to possess the attitude of the Lord Jesus Christ by serving your boss with a positive attitude and be a winner.

2. ***Obedient Lifestyle:*** How we live is critical. Servants with an obedient lifestyle toward God witness the greater blessings of the Lord.

3. ***Servant-Hearted:*** At the heart of every faithful servant is someone who is before God in practice. Being servant-hearted can alter the attitude of the most abusive boss. Having motives of a servant is a plus for both God and Man. Learn to serve with all your heart.

4. ***Sacrificial Spirit:*** In Romans 12:1-2, the Apostle Paul pleads with us who would rather die than sacrifice. Jesus was the ultimate sacrifice to God. He is our example. Learn to sacrifice self for the good of others, including a difficult boss.

 **LIFE JOURNEY**

Personal Life Reflection: What did God say to you today?

_____

_____

_____

_____

_____

_____

_____

The New Journey Prayer using A.C.T.S. (Adoration, Confession, Thanksgiving and Supplication – page 19-20):

1. Do you pray for your boss daily? Do you follow your boss's instructions? Are you an obedient and faithful employee?
2. Ask God to enable you to give your very best effort as an employee.
2. Pray for wisdom before you speak to your boss.
4. Respect your employer's position and obey.

Fast: Abstain from eating three meals and refrain from all types of media.

DAY 37

FOCUS: GOD

Time: _____

Date: _____

Daily Goal:

_____

_____

_____

_____

_____

_____

_____

_____

_____

God's Dress Code

"Gospel peace lifts the Believer above danger."

– William Gurnall,
The Christian in Complete Armour,
Vol. 2, p. 388

LIFE STORY

God's Dress Code:
Put on the Full Armor of God
Read and Meditate: Ephesians 6:10-17

"Put on the full armor of God so that you can stand against the tactics of the Devil" (Eph. 6:11, HCSB).

Dusty stepped into the garage to put out the trash. He knew it was reported from the University of Missouri Climate Center that the winter of 1978-1979 was the coldest winter on record in Missouri during the 20th Century.[7] Despite the warning, Dusty proceeded into the garage without his head and ears properly insulated from the frigid cold. He completed his task in about three to five minutes. However, upon returning to the kitchen, his ears were completely numb, had turned purple and were frostbitten. Dusty learned about the danger of dressing improperly during frigid weather.

When God says, *"Put on the full armor of God so that you can stand against the tactics of the Devil,"* He is not joking. As Christians on *The New Journey* we must realize we are in a spiritual battle for our souls. The Devil desires not only to influence us, but also to exterminate us. Dusty would have never experienced the excruciating, throbbing pain of frostbitten ears if he had been properly dressed. Does your dress meet God's dress code? Do you have your complete armor on as you seek to take your stand against the Devil's tempting tactics? Far too many Christians underdress according to God's divine dress code.

[7]Significant Weather Events of the Century for Missouri, "Coldest Winter of the Century," http://climate.missouri.edu/sigwxmo.php (accessed June 16, 2011).

LIFE PRINCIPLE

Today's Life Principle: *God's Divine Dress Code.* How do we apply this Life Principle on Day 37? By choosing daily to wear the **"Seven Garments in God's Divine Dress Code"**. See if you can select the correct style of each garment:

1. *Truth:*
   [A] Truth is all about me and what I determine to be true.
   [B] Truth is Jesus, *"the way, the truth, and the life."* (John 14:6).

2. *Righteousness:*
   [A] Righteousness is about following God's model.
   [B] Righteousness is something anyone can do.

3. *Peace:*
   [A] Peace with man begins with God first.
   [B] Peace has everything to do with money.

4. *Faith:*
   [A] *"And without faith it is impossible to please God"* (Hebrews 11:6, NIV).
   [B] Without faith, I can still please the Lord Jesus Christ.

5. *Salvation:*
   [A] Salvation means being *"born again"* (John 3:7).
   [B] You can be a Christian without being born again.

6. *Prayer:*
   [A] Prayer is simply spiritual communication to one's minister.
   [B] Prayer is talking to your heavenly Father – God. (Matthew 6:9).

7. *God's Word:*
   [A] God's Word is only for spiritual leaders in the church.
   [B] *"God's Word was made flesh and dwelt among us."* (John 1:14).

All seven are necessary garments for engaging in spiritual warfare. Wear them daily as a follower of Jesus Christ.

LIFE JOURNEY

Personal Life Reflection: What did God say to you today?

_____

_____

_____

_____

_____

_____

_____

The New Journey Prayer using A.C.T.S. (Adoration, Confession, Thanksgiving and Supplication – page 19-20):

1. Believe God that you can be fully dressed and ready for battle.
2. Pray to the Lord and trust His protection at all times. The greater the challenge confronting you, the greater the protection the Lord provides.
3. Understand spiritual warfare is real. Refer to "Scriptures for Fasting" pages 239-244.
4. How are you doing with your prayer list?
5. Have you started a New Journey Small Group Prayer Bible Study?

Fast: Abstain from eating three meals and refrain from all types of media.

DAY 38

FOCUS: GOD

Time: _____

Date: _____

Daily Goal:

_____

_____

_____

_____

_____

_____

_____

_____

_____

_____

God's Spirit

"True prayer is prayer offered to God the Father on the basis of the death of Jesus Christ, His Son."

– James Montgomery Boice, *How to Live the Christian Life*, p. 20

LIFE STORY

God's Divine Communication: Prayer in the Spirit
Read and Meditate: Ephesians 6:18

"*Pray at all times in the Spirit with every prayer and request and stay alert in this with all perseverance and intercession for all the saints*" (Eph. 6:18, HCSB).

At age ten, Madison surrendered her life to Jesus Christ. Her mom and dad spent endless hours teaching her to memorize the "Model Prayer" found in Matthew 6. At age thirteen Madison could recite it impromptu. However, as she matured and grew in the knowledge and wisdom of God, something miraculous materialized out out of her prayer life. Madison experienced "Prayer in the Spirit".

What is "Prayer in the Spirit?" Is it learning to pray in such a manner to manipulate the heart of the Father? Can a person pray and yet fail to pray in the Spirit of God? I believe it is humanly possible to pray in the flesh and completely miss engaging in the precious power found by praying in the Spirit of God. Prayer in the flesh is simply mouthing words. This is prayer devoid of divine power. God hears prayers offered in the flesh, but He is not obligated to respond to them.

"Prayer in the Spirit" occurs when genuine human petitions are sacrificed on the sacred altar of the perfect will of God. It is when the heart of man moves the heart of God. "God accepts the person whose heart is right with His heart."[8] Prayer in the Spirit is Spirit-filled prayer. Is it possible to pray, but not be Spirit-filled?

---

[8]William Gurnall, *The Christian in Complete Armour, Vol. 2*, Abridged by Ruthanne Garlock, Kay King, Karen Sloan and Candy Coan (Carlise, PA: Banner of Truth Trust), 1988, 60.

LIFE PRINCIPLE

Today's Life Principle: *Prayer in the Spirit.* How do we apply this Life Principle on Day 38? By understanding the **"Four Personal Requirements for Praying in the Spirit"**:

1. *Salvation:* No one is capable of praying in the Spirit of God unless he or she has experienced the new birth of salvation. Jesus said to Nicodemus, "*Marvel not that I say unto you, you must be born again*"(John 3:7). What Jesus meant was we must be born from above. There is no substitute for receiving the new birth from above since "above" suggests God's divine involvement. One prerequisite to prayer in the Spirit will always be spiritual new birth.

2. *Holiness:* Holiness is not an activity, but is a state of being. God said, "Be holy." He never called us to be engaged in holy activities. Doing holy activities can be unholy. Personal holiness begins with the individual and God. God comes near and the individual accepts God's invitation to move beyond the new birth to the next level – growing in holiness through Christ.

3. *Communication:* Personal communication is impossible apart from the power and the presence of the Holy Spirit of God. The Holy Spirit is our counselor and guide. He is our prayer coach. When we don't know what to say, He does.

4. *Relationship:* How can one pray in the Spirit if one does not know God through a relationship with Jesus Christ? Knowing God is more than just knowing His name. We must know His heart. Prayer in the Spirit begins and ends with a regenerated heart.

LIFE JOURNEY

Personal Life Reflection: What did God say to you today?

_____

_____

_____

_____

_____

_____

_____

The New Journey Prayer using A.C.T.S. (Adoration, Confession, Thanksgiving and Supplication – page 19-20):

1. When anxious do you pray in the Spirit? Someone has said, "If you worry, then don't pray; but if you pray, then don't worry." Refer to "The Seven Tools of Dealing with Anxiety" pages 249-250.
2. As an intercessory prayer warrior, realize you are able to pray in the Spirit with power, passion and precision. Pray right now and trust God with your request(s).
3. Go back and read your notes to see how far you have come.
4. Have you fasted at least one day using _The New Journey_ approach?

Fast: **Abstain from eating three meals and refrain from all types of media.**

DAY 39

FOCUS: GOD

Time: _____

Date: _____

Daily Goal:

_____

_____

_____

_____

_____

_____

_____

_____

_____

_____

Deep, Deep Love

"Love of the brethren arises from the love of the Father."

– Andrew Murray, *An Exciting New Life*, p. 77

LIFE STORY

God's Deep Love:
Pray for One Another – Intercession
Read and Meditate: Ephesians 6:18-20

"With every prayer and request…with all perseverance and intercession... Pray also for me..." (Eph. 6:18-19a).

The ministry of intercession is an awe-inspiring ministry of prayer. I vividly remember my wife praying for me in one of the darkest days of my ministry and service as a local pastor. I recall her placing a Bible on my head and then on my heart as she cried out to the Lord God Almighty to deliver me from the tactics, tricks and temptations of the spirit of Lucifer. I am unable to recount every last word of her intercessory prayer, but I am confident that my Heavenly Father accepted her intercessory "Prayer in the Spirit" on my behalf. My wife provided deep, deep love – the agapé love of God.

Deep love is best illustrated in intercessory prayer. My wife loved me through intercessory prayer and taught me what deep agapé love of Christ looked like. Agapé Love perseveres through all heartaches, hardships and situations. I must say, until I received Jesus Christ as my Savior and Lord, I had never known such love. Whenever someone intercedes on your behalf, it is an expression of Christ's deep agapé love. Even a blind man can recognize this kind of love. I am so grateful my wife prayed for me, but most of all, I am eternally grateful Jesus died for me at Calvary as an expression of His agapé love. Why should we as individuals and as a church engage in intercessory prayer? To show deep agapé love to others.

LIFE PRINCIPLE ✗

Today's Life Principle: *The Prayer of Intercession.* How do we apply this Life Principle on Day 39? By engaging individually and corporately in the **"Four Spheres of Intercessory Prayer"**:

1. *The Jerusalem Sphere:* Jesus instructed the disciples in the final chapter of Luke to go back to Jerusalem and wait for the promised Holy Spirit of God. Just as the Lord had promised and prophesied, His promise arrived right on time in the form of the Holy Spirit. As we intercede and pray in the Spirit for others, start at home.

2. *The Judea Sphere:* The excitement of the arrival of the promised Holy Spirit blazed across the landscape of the city of Jerusalem until it bubbled over to the second sphere, Judea. God's Holy Spirit freely spread as the Lord had promised. The supernatural movement of the Spirit of God could not be contained. As we intercede and pray in the Spirit for others, don't stop at home. Spread into praying for our neighborhood.

3. *The Samaria Sphere:* Next, the Spirit spilled over into the northern city of Samaria. Samaritans were called half-breeds and looked down upon by the full-bred Jewish establishment. The Holy Spirit still moved and whoever's heart became open to the Gospel of Jesus Christ was saved! As we intercede and pray in the Spirit, remember to pray for coworkers and friends who need Jesus.

4. *The Uttermost Sphere: "With every prayer and request... with all perseverance and intercession... Pray also for me..."* (Ephesians 6:18-19a, HCSB). From Jerusalem to Judea to Samaria to the uttermost parts of the world, this was God's plan of intercessory prayer in the Spirit. Let us make God's plan our plan and pray while interceding in the Spirit, for our world.

LIFE JOURNEY

Personal Life Reflection: What did God say to you today?

_____

_____

_____

_____

_____

_____

_____

_____

The New Journey Prayer using A.C.T.S. (Adoration, Confession, Thanksgiving and Supplication – page 19-20):

1. Ask God to help you make and maintain your own intercessory prayer list using *The New Journey* template on pages 259-260. You are free to make copies of the prayer list page to strengthen and expand your intercessory prayer list.

2. Discover ways to pray for other Christians as well as unbelievers.

3. Did you fast today as instructed?

Fast: **Abstain from eating food, viewing all media and talking for 24 hours. Pray for revival and spiritual awakening.**

DAY 40

FOCUS: GOD

Time: _____

Date: _____

Daily Goal:

_____

_____

_____

_____

_____

_____

_____

_____

_____

_____

Godly Determination

"When Mr. Steadfast had thus set things in order, and time being come for him to haste, there was a great calm at that time in the River..."

– John Bunyan, *The Pilgrim's Progress*, p. 377

LIFE STORY

Tychicus:
A Determined Encourager
Read and Meditate: Ephesians 6:21- 24

"Tychicus... I am sending him to you... to let you know how we are and to encourage your hearts" (Eph. 6:21a-22, HCSB).

Encouragement and comfort are always welcomed traveling companions on *The New Journey*. Success on the journey is often determined by one's traveling companions. Blackie was Walter's traveling companion. Almost everywhere he traveled, Blackie was with him. Until one day, Blackie was struck by a speeding vehicle and died. Blackie was a Labrador Retriever and will always be remembered as Walter's encouragement and comfort. His comfort and encouragement died when Blackie died.

Tychicus was commissioned by the Apostle Paul to carry out at least two assignments. He was to inform Believers of the Gospel's progress in the lives of faithful Christians scattered throughout Asia Minor and beyond. Tychicus was also to encourage fellow Believers to continue in their faith despite Roman oppression, religious hypocrisy and Satanic warfare. Tychicus provided the Believers what the Lord provides for us today: comfort and encouragement through the Holy Spirit, God's Comforter (John 14). As we continue on the path of *The New Journey*, let us never forget we have the same Comforter and Encourager traveling along with us. Think. When was the last time we encouraged someone or someone encouraged us in the Spirit of God?

LIFE PRINCIPLE ✂

Today's Life Principle: *Encouragement.* How do we apply this Life Principle on Day 40? By discovering **"Five Distinct Ways of Encouraging the Heart of Fellow Believers"**:

1. Employ the three fundamental types of affirmation; personal, private and corporate.
   - *Personal Affirmation* addresses others on an individual basis. God uses us to strengthen others for however long is necessary.
   - *Private Affirmation* is done covertly and often occurs in mission fields hostile to the Gospel. If the affirmed community were identified, their lives would be in jeopardy, so private affirmation is done only in unique situations.
   - *Corporate Affirmation* strengthens the larger body of Christ. It might occur within one church body or a number of churches congregating together to sharpen the work of the Kingdom of God.

2. Perform random acts of kindness.

3. Practice hospitality by inviting someone to a meal in your home.

4. Share a hobby with someone who needs encouragment.

5. Make others aware you are praying on a daily basis for them and their family.

 LIFE JOURNEY

Personal Life Reflection: What did God say to you today?

_____

_____

_____

_____

_____

_____

The New Journey Prayer using A.C.T.S. (Adoration, Confession, Thanksgiving and Supplication – page 19-20):

1. Make a commitment to be a godly encourager to Christians on the frontline of Spiritual warfare. See page 244 on "Breaking Spiritual Strongholds."

2. Start an intercessory prayer ministry to encourage your pastor, his staff and leaders.

3. Pray that the Lord Jesus Christ will create within you a spirit of encouragement like Tychicus. Refer to pages 256-258 and highlight the "CTJ" passages in your Bible.

4. How many days did you participate in a fast as suggested by _The New Journey_.

Fast: Abstain from eating one meal and read your Bible for three hours.

REFLECTIONS

Peaks and Valleys: Concluding the 40 Days

Congratulations!!! You have made it. You have completed your *New Journey*. Your commitment level has been awesome. You are to be praised for a job well done. However, you are not finished. Why? The Christian is never completely whole or holy until the day we see Jesus face-to-face. It will be a glorious day when our Lord and Savior Jesus Christ returns. I can't wait to be there with you and all of my fellow travelers on the Christian journey. What a day of rejoicing it will be.

So let's turn our attention to concluding our present journey What I would like for you to do is to take about 30 minutes and pause to reflect over your *New Journey*. What did God say to you? What things did you see and/or experience during your journey? Did you experience some deep changes in your life? Were you challenged to live more obediently to God? To what peaks did you soar or to what valleys did you descend? What did you learn about yourself and your personal relationship with Almighty God?

This is your opportunity to do a little introspective prodding. You may be surprised what you will find once you begin to turn over a few covered rocks and stones in your life. Roll up your sleeves, grit your teeth, press pen or pencil to paper and write about your peaks and valleys. Go for it. Give it all you've got. You have nothing to lose. Enjoy! It's okay to have a little fun. The Lord does not mind you embracing a frolicking spirit. It's your time now. Reflect! Use the next few pages to write your reflective stories.

UPWARD: The Peak

The New Journey: UPWARD - The Peak

DOWNWARD: The Valley

The New Journey: DOWNWARD - The Valley

FINAL REFLECTIONS

APPENDIX I

Small Group New Journey Study

PrayerDiscipleship™ Groups

PrayerDiscipleship™ Groups are the key to helping strengthen and expand the ministry of the local church. Next Level PrayerDiscipleship™ is what every church, new work, church plant, traditional church or developing and expanding church community needs. *The New Journey* is not simply a prayer devotional journal but also a PrayerDiscipleship™ devotional journal. Far too many churches, small groups, community fellowship and existing congregations do an excellent job in discipleship, but fail greatly in the ministry of prayer. When prayer and discipleship are merged into one strategy, newer and healthier Christian disciples emerge. This is the goal of *The New Journey* – Prayer Disciples.

How is this achieved? Through encouraging emerging (i.e., maturing) Prayer Disciples to learn how to manage their struggles and maximize their strengths. Learning from the Life Stories, applying the Life Principles and living out the Life Journeys produces Prayer Disciples. *The New Journey* can begin anytime, but growing as a Prayer Disciple requires fellowship with other disciples in community. Community comes through intentional small groups.

The Small Group Study comprises eight lessons. Each small group lesson is structured in a similar way and consists of five days of reflection upon topics in *The New Journey*.

Lesson 1: Day 2 – Day 5

1. Review the **"Seven Critical Truths"** that can cancel every traveler's fear from Day 2

2. Discuss the **"Ten Commandments"** a fearless traveler follows to overcome fear from Day 3.

3. Look at the **"15 Progressive Stages of Spiritual Growth"** as we emerge from a pit from Day 4.

4. Have you ever experienced life in the pit? What was it like? What did you do to get out of your pit?

5. Define grace and mercy as discussed on Day 5.

Lesson 1: Response

_____

_____

_____

_____

_____

_____

_____

_____

Lesson 1: Response

_____

_____

_____

_____

_____

_____

_____

_____

_____

_____

_____

_____

_____

_____

_____

_____

_____

_____

_____

Lesson 2: Day 6 – Day 10

1. Discuss the **"Nine Requirements of an Effective Prayer Ministry"** from Day 6. Does your church have an effective prayer ministry? Why or why not?

2. Consider the **"40 Traits of a Modern Day Nehemiah"** from Day 7. Which traits best depict you? Which traits do you need to sharpen or embrace?

3. Identify the **"Five Levels of Hope"** from Day 8. Which level do you feel you are on at this time in your life?

4. Identify the **"Top Ten Symptoms of Divorcing God"** from Day 9. Does your church possess any of these symptoms? Remember there is no perfect church and there are no perfect people.

5. Think about whether you have any "kryptonite" in your life mentioned in Day 10 which is hindering you from soaring higher for the Lord.

Lesson 2: Response

_____

_____

_____

_____

_____

_____

_____

Lesson 2: Response

_____

_____

_____

_____

_____

_____

_____

_____

_____

_____

_____

_____

_____

_____

_____

_____

_____

Lesson 3: Day 11 – Day 15

1. Where in the Bible will you find the Lord's Prayer as mentioned on Day 11?

2. Discuss the **"Seven Requirements of a Life that is Sanctified by Truth"** from Day 12.

3. What did you learn from Christopher's life story on Day 13?

4. Review the **"Seven Ingredients in a Steadfast Prayer Life"** from Day 14.

5. Are you sharing your Christian faith in any of your Four Relational Circles mentioned on Day 15? How consistent are you in sharing your faith? If you are not persistent, why?

Lesson 3: Response

_____

_____

_____

_____

_____

_____

_____

_____

Lesson 3: Response

_____

_____

_____

_____

_____

_____

_____

_____

_____

_____

_____

_____

_____

_____

_____

_____

_____

_____

_____

_____

_____

Lesson 4: Day 16 – Day 20

1. What was Zoe's problem on Day 16? What did Butch do to help his wife?

2. Discuss the **"Four B's"** in becoming an imitator of Christ from Day 17.

3. Name, discuss and spend time in prayer concerning your church growing deeper and expressing moe of the **"Nine Marks of a Godly Christian Character"** on Day 18.

4. Review the **"Five Deadliest Lies about the Truth"** on Day 19.

5. Identify the **"Five Positive Sides of Anger"** on Day 20.

Lesson 4: Response

_____

_____

_____

_____

_____

_____

_____

_____

Lesson 4: Response

_____

_____

_____

_____

_____

_____

_____

_____

_____

_____

_____

_____

_____

_____

_____

_____

_____

_____

_____

_____

Lesson 5: Day 21 – Day 25

1. Review the **"Ten Ways Our Behavior Mirrors Our Belief"** on Day 21.

2. Consider the **"Five Impacts of a Godly Christian Leader of the Church"** from Day 22.

3. Name the **"Nine Abundant Fruiuts of the Christian's Heart"** discussed on Day 23. How much fruit are you producing?

4. Name, discuss and pray about your church's need to model the **"Four Demonstrations of Living Agapé"** on Day 24.

5. Prayerfully read Day 25's **Life Principle** on *Forgiveness* and discuss what forgiveness can do for a church, a marriage, a relationship and a person's life.

Lesson 5: Response

_____

_____

_____

_____

_____

_____

_____

_____

Lesson 5: Response

Lesson 6: Day 26 – Day 30

1. Review the **"Four Things the Light of God Refuses to Force Us to Do"** on Day 26.

2. What did you learn about Pastor Loggins' mother, Gladys Louise Loggins, on Day 27?

3. Discuss the **"Four Steps to Developing a Winning Walk of Wisdom"** on Day 28. Share one you struggle with the most.

4. According to Day 29's **Life Story** teaching, what is Spirit-filled living?

5. Discuss the personalities in Day 30's **Life Principle** on Christian talk. What have you done to avoid unhealthy Christian communication?

Lesson 6: Response

_____

_____

_____

_____

_____

_____

_____

_____

Lesson 6: Response

_____

_____

_____

_____

_____

_____

_____

_____

_____

_____

_____

_____

_____

_____

_____

_____

_____

_____

_____

Lesson 7: Day 31 – Day 35

1. Review the **"Three Christian Expressions of Fearful Submission"** on Day 31. Are you a biblically submissive person?

2. Consider the **"Four Beginnings of a Bad Marriage"** on Day 32. How have you avoided any of these beginnings in your marriage?

3. How do we deal with the **"Four Historical Wounds of a Wounded Marriage"** found on Day 33?

4. Discuss the **"Four Keys of Appreciation for Both Worthy and Unworthy Parents"** on Day 34.

5. Identify the **"Four Gems in the Life of Every Child"** on Day 35.

Lesson 7: Response

_____

_____

_____

_____

_____

_____

_____

_____

Lesson 7: Response

_____

_____

_____

_____

_____

_____

_____

_____

_____

_____

_____

_____

_____

_____

_____

_____

_____

_____

Lesson 8: Day 36 – Day 40

1. Discuss the **"Four Non-Negotiable Behaviors of a Faithful Servant"** on Day 36. How do you practice these behaviors in spite of a difficult boss?

2. Read Ephesians 6:10-20 and discuss how to dress for spiritual warfare as described on Day 37. Are you usually dressed properly for spiritual warfare?

3. What does it require for an individual to **"Pray in Spirit"** of God according to Day 38?

4. Identify the **"Four Spheres of Intercessory Prayer"** listed on Day 39 in which all churches are commissioned by God to engage.

5. Review the **"Five Distinct Ways of Encouraging the Heart of a Fellow Believer"** on Day 40. How have you encouraged a brother or sister in Christ this week?

Lesson 8: Response

_____

_____

_____

_____

_____

_____

_____

_____

Lesson 8: Response

_____

_____

_____

_____

_____

_____

_____

_____

_____

_____

_____

_____

_____

_____

_____

_____

_____

_____

_____

APPENDIX II

Guide to Fasting and Prayer

Seven Basic Steps to Successful Fasting and Prayer, written by Bill Bright © 1995 Bright Media Foundation and Campus Crusade for Christ International. All rights reserved.

(No part of this work may be included in another work or placed on a website without written permission. http://www.brightmedia.org. Used with permission.)

Your Personal Guide to Fasting and Prayer

The Dynamic Purposes for Fasting and Praying:

1. To help equip the Saints of God for a deeper walk with God for the edification of the Lord Jesus Christ (Eph. 4:11-16).
2. To address a "this kind of spirit" (Mark 9).
3. To break bondages (OT, Declaration of times of Fasting and Praying).
4. To develop intimacy with our Heavenly Father.
5. To grow deeper in our faith, love, and commitment to the cause of Christ.
6. To change the unspiritual or the ungodly or the irreverent to the righteousness of God.
7. To change what is to what God would have it to be ("...and we shall be changed...")

Fasting is the most powerful spiritual discipline of all the Christian disciplines. Through fasting and prayer, the Holy Spirit can transform your life.

Fasting and prayer can also work on a much grander scale. According to Scripture, personal experience and observation, I am convinced that when God's people fast with a proper Biblical motive-seeking God's face not His hand-with a broken, repentant, and contrite spirit, God will hear from heaven and heal our lives, our churches, our communities, our nation and world. Fasting and prayer can bring about revival – a change in the direction of our nation, the nations of earth and the fulfillment of the Great Commission.

Seven Basic Steps to Successful Fasting and Prayer, written by Bill Bright © 1995 Bright Media Foundation and Campus Crusade for Christ International. All rights reserved. No part of this work may be included in another work or placed on a website without written permission. http://www.brightmedia.org. Used with permission.

The awesome power can be released through you as you fast through the enabling of the Holy Spirit.

Fasting is one of the most neglected spiritual admonitions. In fact, it has been ignored for so long that it is difficult to find information on the "how-to's" of this life-changing experience. When I first undertook an extended fast, I had a difficult time finding information on the nature of a Biblical fast, how to start, what to expect physically and spiritually, and how to terminate a fast.

These pages are designed to answer your practical questions about fasting and ease any concerns you might have. In this series, you will learn:

- Why you should fast
- How to fast safely
- How long and what type of fast is right for you
- How to prepare yourself spiritually and physically
- How to manage your schedule while fasting
- How to deal with the responses of friends and loved ones
- How to make your spiritual experience the best it can be
- How to maintain nutritional balance and health from beginning to end (including specific juice and broth recipes)
- What physical benefits to expect
- How to finish your fast and return to your normal schedule in a HEALTHY way

I want to be of help to you so I will be speaking to you from these pages at various points in the study. I have completed five 40-day fasts. I want to share with you what I have learned and what has helped me. Whether you hold a 1-day fast or an extended 40-day fast, I pray that our Lord's most wonderful love and blessings will be poured out on you as you take this exciting step of faith.

Why You Should Fast

If you do not already know of the power and importance of fasting, here are some very important facts:

- Fasting was an expected discipline in both the Old and New Testament eras. For example, Moses fasted at least two recorded forty-day periods. Jesus fasted 40 days and reminded His followers to fast, "when you fast," not if you fast.
- Fasting and prayer can restore the loss of the "first love" for your Lord and result in a more intimate relationship with Christ.
- Fasting is a biblical way to truly humble yourself in the sight of God (Psalm 35:13; Ezra 8:21). King David said, "I humble myself through fasting."
- Fasting enables the Holy Spirit to reveal your true spiritual condition, resulting in brokenness, repentance, and a transformed life.
- The Holy Spirit will quicken the Word of God in your heart and His truth will become more meaningful to you!
- Fasting can transform your prayer life into a richer and more personal experience.
- Fasting can result in a dynamic personal revival in your own life- and make you a channel of revival to others.
- Fasting and prayer are the only disciplines that fulfill the requirements of II Chronicles 7:14:
  "If my people, who are called by my name, will humble themselves and pray and seek my face and turn from their wicked ways, then will I hear from heaven and will forgive their sin and will heal their land."

If you fast, you will find yourself being humbled as I did. You will discover more time to pray and seek God's face. And as He leads you to recognize and repent of unconfessed sin, you will experience special blessings from God.

How to Fast Safely

As you begin your fast, you may hear from concerned loved ones and friends who urge you to protect your health. And they are right. You should protect your health. But I assure you, if done properly, fasting will not only prove to be a spiritual blessing, but physical blessing as well.

By all means, consult your doctor before you begin your fast. But, be aware that many doctors have not been trained in this area and so their understanding is limited. Even so, it would be wise to ask your doctor for a physical exam to make sure you are in good health. You may have a physical problem that would make fasting unwise or dangerous. Also, if you are under any type of medication, make sure you talk to your doctor before changing your regime. Prudence and caution are in order.

When you are assured that you are in good health, you are ready to begin your fast. Follow the guidelines in the Physical Preparations and Maintaining Nutritional Balance and Health parts of this website.

In spite of the absolute safety and benefits of fasting, there are certain persons who should NEVER fast without professional supervision. For example:

- Persons who are physically too thin or emaciated.
- Persons who are prone to anorexia, bulimia, or other behavioral disorders.
- Those who suffer weakness or anemia.
- Persons who have tumors, bleeding ulcers, cancer, blood diseases, or who have heart disease.
- Those who suffer chronic problems with kidneys, liver, lungs, heart, or other important organs.
- Individuals who take insulin for diabetes, or suffer any other blood sugar problem such as hyperglycemia.
- Women who are pregnant or nursing.

Seven Basic Steps to Successful Fasting and Prayer, written by Bill Bright © 1995 Bright Media Foundation and Campus Crusade for Christ International. All rights reserved. No part of this work may be included in another work or placed on a website without written permission. http://www.brightmedia.org. Used with permission.

How Long and What Type of Fast is Right for You

If you have never fasted before, I applaud your present interest! Fasting has been a major emphasis in the lives of many of the great spiritual leaders throughout history. John Wesley, the founder of the Methodist denomination, fasted every Wednesday and Friday and required all of his clergy to do the same. Effective ministers of God from the apostle Paul to Martin Luther to John Calvin made it a continual part of their walks with God.

None of those men had a "formula fast" that was the only "right" way. Fasting is about the condition of the heart, not the number of days. Each time that I have fasted for forty days, it was because I felt impressed by God to do so.

So, start slowly. Fast for one meal a day, or one day a week, or one week a month. Build up your spiritual muscles so that you will be prepared in a period of several months to fast for an extended 40 day period.

The Bible Recounts Primarily Two Types of Fasts

A partial fast is described in the book of Daniel. Although the water fast seemed to be the custom of the prophet, there was a three-week period in which he only abstained from "delicacies," meat, and wine (Daniel 10:3).

The two primary types mentioned in the Bible are the "absolute" and "supernatural absolute" fasts. These are total fasts-no food (solid or liquid) and no water. Paul went on an absolute fast for three days following his encounter with Jesus on the road to Damascus (Acts 9:9). Moses and Elijah engaged in what must be considered a supernatural absolute fast of forty days (Deuteronomy 9:9; I Kings 19:8). So, I strongly advise you to drink plenty of liquids.

Obviously, if God leads you to undertake an absolute fast, you should obey. If so, be certain, without doubt, that God is leading you.

Water-only fasts that last for more than several days need to be undertaken with complete rest and under medical supervision because of the extreme danger of over-toxification, breakdown of vital body tissues, and loss of electrolytes.

I personally recommend and practice water and juice fasting, especially if you are going to fast for an extended period of time. This type of fast will provide you with more energy than absolute or water-only fasts and still lead you into the humbling experience of denying your desire for solid food that you can chew.

When it comes to making your final decision about what type of fast is right for you, the best advice I can give you is to follow the leading of the Holy Spirit. He will guide your heart and mind as to what is best for you. Remember, the most important consideration in fasting is your motive. Why are you fasting? To seek something personally from God's hand or to seek His face in worship, praise and thanksgiving?

Spiritual Preparation

In preparation for this special time with God, I strongly urge you to examine your heart, and detect any unconfessed sin. Scripture records that God always requires His people to repent of their sins before He will hear their prayers. King David said:

Come and hear, all of you who reverence the Lord, and I will tell you what he did for me: For I cried to him for help, with praises ready on my tongue. He would not have listened if I had not confessed my sins. But he listened! He heard my prayer! He paid attention to it!

Blessed be God who didn't turn away when I was praying, and didn't refuse me his kindness and love. (Psalm 66:16-20)

In your prayers, confess not only obvious sins, but less obvious ones as well. That is the sins of omission as well as the sins of commission experiences. These may be experiences leaving your first love for our Lord: worldly-mindedness, self-centeredness, spiritual indifference, and unwillingness to share your faith in Christ with others, not spending sufficient time in God's Word and in prayer, a poor relationship with your spouse, your children, your pastor, or other members of your church.

Another great way to prepare for your fast is to practice what I call "Spiritual Breathing." The concept is simple, but it has changed my own life and that of millions of others.

Like physical breathing, Spiritual Breathing is a process of exhaling the impure and inhaling the pure. If you knowingly sin, breathe spiritually to restore the fullness of God's Holy Spirit in your life. You exhale by confessing your sins immediately when you become aware of them, and you inhale by inviting the Holy Spirit to re-take control of your life. As an act of faith, trust Him to empower you. During the fast, spiritual breathing-constant reliance on the Holy Spirit will enable you to resist temptation, not only to sin but to abandon your fast.

Physical Preparation

Although fasting is primarily a spiritual discipline, it begins in the physical realm. You should not fast without specific physical preparation.

If you plan on fasting for several days, you will find it helpful to begin by eating smaller meals before you abstain altogether. Resist the urge to have that "last big feast" before the fast. Cutting down on your meals a few days before you begin the fast will signal your mind, stomach, and appetite that less food is acceptable.

Some health professionals suggest eating only raw foods for two days before starting a fast. I also recommend weaning yourself off caffeine and sugar products to ease your initial hunger or discomfort at the early stages of your fast.

How to Manage Your Schedule While Fasting

How long you fast, the kind of fast you undertake, and how you adjust your work schedule depends mostly on your occupation. Persons with office jobs, pastors, or homemakers may find it easier to continue their duties and fast for longer periods of time. In fact, on the basis of my personal experience, worldwide travels and the many letters, which I have received, I am confident that many, many thousands of pastors and lay men and women have already completed a 40-day fast!

Though there are many who engage in strenuous physical labor and have enjoyed their extended fast, if you are so engaged, you may wish to fast only one or more days of the week, limiting yourselves to partial fasting if you are so engaged. Or you may look to weekends as the prime time to abstain from food. Remember, too, fasting during major holidays is not always a good idea. Families may be inconvenienced, and temptations to eat can be overwhelming.

Reasons for schedule adjustments, especially during an extended fast, are two-fold...

The first reason is physical...

Throughout your fast, you may feel somewhat weaker than normal. During the first few days, you may feel tired and irritable. Lightening your workload and cutting down on strenuous exercise would be a very good idea to maintain your health and your morale.

The second reason is spiritual...

Fasting is not just denying yourself food. It is exchanging the needs of the physical body for those of the spiritual. Long times of prayer and reading God's Word will be very essential if you are to enter into a more intimate communion with God to maintain your fast to its completion.

While fasting, if you dissipate your energy on numerous errands or busy-work to the neglect of spending special time with God, you will starve both physically and spiritually. You will find yourself becoming discouraged and frustrated with your fast instead of being benefited and uplifted and blessed. I don't want that to happen to you.

The more time you spend with God in fellowship, worship, and adoration of Him, and the more you read and meditate upon His Word, the greater your effectiveness will be in prayer and the more meaningful your fast will be. So I encourage you to arrange your schedule accordingly!

Dealing With the Responses of Friends and Loved Ones

Many people are reluctant to tell others that they are fasting so they will avoid the sin of the Pharisees: fasting just to gain recognition for themselves. I strongly believe that attitude is a result of a wrong interpretation of our Lord's teaching and that it is a trick of the enemy who does not want us to fast, nor to share with your loved ones, neighbors and friends the benefits of fasting.

By isolating ourselves from the support of other Christians, we will be more susceptible to doubts and negative influences (both human and demonic). We need the prayer shield of our Christian friends and family members to help us continue when we feel alone and when the enemy tempts us to give up Our Lord as he did Jesus Christ. Eventually, people will notice you are not eating.

However, I have found that unless you see them daily, they do not consider your skipped meal much of a concern. If you are asked, nonbelievers may be satisfied by such a brief answer as, "I have other plans for lunch today." Or Christians should be satisfied when you answer that you are fasting today.

If friends and family express concern for your health, ease their fears by telling them that you will stop fasting the moment you feel you are harming your body or if the Lord leads you to end your fast. Tell them you are fasting under your doctor's care, which I urge you to do if you have any question concerning your health.

There is usually no reason for telling strangers or casual acquaintances you are fasting. If you do, they may subject you to a lot of questions that you may not want to answer. But in any case, use your best judgment and the Lord's leading in telling people about your fast.

213

How to Make Your Spiritual Experience the Best it Can Be

Receiving God's best blessing from a fast requires solid commitment. Arranging special time each day with God is absolutely crucial in attaining intimate communion with the Father. You must devote yourself to seeking God's face, even (and especially) during those times in which you feel weak, vulnerable, or irritable. Read His Word and pray during what were mealtimes. Meditate on Him when you awake in the night. Sing praises to Him whenever you please. Focus on your Heavenly Father and make every act one of praise and worship. God will enable you to experience His command to "pray without ceasing" as you seek His presence.

As you enter this time of heightened spiritual devotion, be aware that Satan will do everything he can to pull you away from your prayer and Bible reading time. When you feel the enemy trying to discourage you, immediately go to God in prayer and ask Him to strengthen your resolve in the face of difficulties and temptations.

The enemy makes you a target because he knows that fasting is the most powerful of all Christian disciplines and that God may have something very special to show you as you wait upon Him and seek His face. Satan does not want you to grow in your faith, and will do anything from making you hungry and grumpy to bringing up trouble in your family or at work to stop you. Make prayer your shield against such attacks.

My major reason for fasting is for personal revival, revival for our nation, for the world and for the fulfillment of the Great Commission by the end of the year 2000. But praying for our own needs and interceding for others are also important reasons to fast and pray. Bring your personal needs before the Lord; intercede for your loved ones, your friends, your church, your pastor, your community, your nation, and the world. By your prayers of humility, as you fast, you will help the Great Commission be fulfilled.

However, do not become so caught up in praying for yourself and others that you forget about simply reverencing and praising God. True spiritual fasting focuses on God. Center your total being on Him, your attitudes, your actions, your motives, desires, and words. This can only take place if God and His Holy Spirit are at the center of our attention. Confess your sins as the Holy Spirit brings them to your attention and continue to focus on God and God alone so that your prayers may be powerful and effective.

A renewed closeness with God and a greater sensitivity to spiritual things are usually the results of a fast. Do not be disappointed if you do not have a "mountaintop experience," as some do. Many people who have successfully completed extended fasts tell of feeling a nearness to God that they have never before known, but others who have honestly sought His face report no particular outward results at all. For others, their fast was physically, emotionally, and spiritually grueling, but they knew they had been called by God to fast, and they completed the fast unto Him as an act of worship; God honored that commitment.

Your motive in fasting must be to glorify God, not to have an emotional experience, and not to attain personal happiness. When your motives are right, God will honor your seeking heart and bless your time with Him in a very special way.

How to Maintain Nutritional Balance and Health from Beginning to End

I know the prospect of going without food for an extended period of time may be of concern to some. But there are ways to ensure that your body is getting the nutrients it needs so you can remain safe and healthy during your fast.

For an extended fast, I recommend water and fruit and vegetable juices. The natural sugars in juices provide energy, and the taste and strength are motivational to continue your fast. Try to drink fresh juices, if possible. Off-the-shelf juice products are acceptable, as long as they are 100% juice with no sugar or other additives.

If you are beginning a juice fast, there are certain juices you may wish to avoid and certain ones that are especially beneficial. Because of their acid content, most nutritionists do not advise orange or tomato juice (these are better tolerated if mixed with equal portions of water). The best juices are fresh carrot, grape, celery, apple, cabbage, or beet. They also recommend "green drinks" made from green leafy vegetables because they are excellent "de-toxifiers."

Fruit juices are "cleansers" and are best taken in the morning. Since vegetable juices are "restorers" and "builders," they are best taken in the afternoon.

I usually dedicate a portion of my 40-day fast to a special liquid formula, which I have found to be effective over many years. A few recipes and my comments are on this page, as well as a helpful schedule.

- One gallon distilled water
- 1-1/2 cup lemon juice
- 3/4-cup pure maple syrup
- 1/4-teaspoon cayenne pepper.

The lemon juice adds flavor and vitamin C, the maple syrup provides energy, and the cayenne pepper – an herb – acts to open small blood vessels which, I believe, helps the body as it cleanses itself of stored toxins. (A word of caution: although I use this formula with no ill effects, cayenne pepper could cause severe physical reactions in persons with a specific allergy to this herb.)

My favorite juice is a mixture of 100% pure white grape juice and peach juice. The juice is available in frozen cans under the Welch label. Most knowledgeable nutritionists recommend:

- Watermelon -- just put it in the blender without adding water
- Fresh apple juice
- Green juice -- blend celery, romaine lettuce, and carrots in equal proportions. (Vegetable juices like this one are important, for they supply the electrolytes necessary for proper heart function!)

Some nutritionists recommend warm broth, especially if you live in a colder climate. You may find their recipes helpful:

- Boil sliced potatoes, carrots, and celery in water. Do not add salt. After about a half-hour, drain off the water and drink.
- Gently boil three carrots, two stalks of celery, one turnip, two beats, a half head of cabbage, a quarter of a bunch of parsley, a quarter of an onion, and a half clove of garlic
- Drain off the broth and drink up to two or three times daily.

You may find the following daily schedule helpful during your fast. I recommend you print it and keep it handy throughout your fast.

- 5:00 a.m. - 8:00 a.m. – Fruit juices, preferably freshly squeezed or blended, diluted in 50 percent distilled water if the fruit is acid. Orange, apple, pear, grapefruit, papaya, grape, peach or other fruits are good.
- 10:30 a.m. - noon – Green vegetable juice made from lettuce, celery, and carrots in three equal parts.
- 2:30 p.m. - 4:00 p.m. – Herb tea with a drop of honey. Make sure that it is not black tea or tea with a stimulant.
- 6:00 p.m. - 8:30 p.m. – Broth from boiled potatoes, celery, and carrots (no salt).

I suggest that you do not drink milk because it is a pure food and therefore a violation of the fast. Any product containing protein or fat, such as milk or soy-based drinks, should be avoided. These products will restart the digestion cycle and you will again feel hunger pangs. Also, for health reasons stay away from caffeinated beverages such as coffee, tea, or cola. Because caffeine is a stimulant, it has a more powerful effect on your nervous system when you abstain from food. This works both against the physical and spiritual aspects of the fast.

Another key factor in maintaining optimum health during a fast is to limit your physical activity. Exercise only moderately, and rest as much as your schedule will permit (this especially applies to extended fasts). Short naps are helpful as well. Walking a mile or two each day at a moderate pace is acceptable for a person in good health, and on a juice fast. However, no one on a water fast should exercise without the supervision of a fasting specialist.

What Physical Effects to Expect

Although fasting can be an indescribable blessing, it is not always easy for everyone. In this time of discipline, self-sacrifice and reflection do not be surprised if you experience mental and physical discomforts.

To begin, you may experience some inner conflict when you deny yourself the pleasure of eating delicious food. Any sort of fast may sometimes leave you feeling impatient and irritable. During a 3-day fast, this struggle can intensify toward the end of the second day. That seems to be a favorite time for the "self" to rise up and say, "This is as far as I want to go. I have done enough."

Physical Effect

- Hunger Pangs: These are greatest usually during the first three days of the fast. Your body is adjusting from using the food in your digestive tract (which remains about three days) to consuming stored fats.

Suggested Relief

- Psyllium Bulk: Help eliminate hunger pangs and also aids in cleansing the body. Several capsules can be taken throughout the day with plenty of water.

- Silymarin tablets may also be helpful, for they are believed to protect and enhance the cleansing of the liver.

Physical Effect

- Coldness, bad breath and heightened body odor, changes in elimination (constipation or diarrhea), light-headedness, changes in sleeping and dreaming patterns, aches and pains.

Seven Basic Steps to Successful Fasting and Prayer, written by Bill Bright © 1995 Bright Media Foundation and Campus Crusade for Christ International. All rights reserved. No part of this work may be included in another work or placed on a website without written permission. http://www.brightmedia.org. Used with permission.

- A white-coated tongue at the beginning of a fast may be a part of the body's pattern of throwing off toxins.

- Also expect to go to the bathroom often (you will be drinking lots of water!)

Suggested Relief

- After the first two weeks of an extended fast, many of these symptoms subside. Continuing aches in a certain area of the body usually means elimination of fatty tissue is going on in that area, which is not harmful. However, any extensive pain should be examined immediately.

- YOU SHOULD STOP FASTING IF YOU ARE EXPERIENCING SEVERE PAIN OR SWELLING.

Physical Effect

- Headaches or stomachaches may be a result of salt, sugar, or caffeine withdrawal.

Suggested Relief

- Eliminating those items from your diet prior to fasting is the best way to avoid these pains.

Physical Effect

- Lower back pain may indicate that you are dehydrating.

Suggested Relief

- Drink more fluids.

Physical Effect

- Dizziness may be caused by a sudden change in position, such as rising suddenly from a chair.

Suggested Relief

- Stop for a second or two, and then recover. Move slowly. (A word of caution: these conditions may be symptoms of other problems requiring medical attention).

Physical Effect

- Minor fasting discomfort

Suggested Relief

- Take one teaspoon of psyllium seed powder morning and evening. Mixed in lukewarm water, it becomes like Jell-O. This powder will hasten the elimination of toxins from your colon and help to prevent headaches and dizziness for most healthy people. Alfalfa tablets can help control bad breath and cleanse the system. Two tablets at a time can be taken several times a day.

In my desire to be absolutely faithful to my first 40-day fast, I stopped taking my usual vitamins and minerals. However during subsequent fasts, I have felt strongly impressed to continue my vitamin and herbal therapy and also using psyllium. I do this to keep my "temple" healthy while continuing to deny myself the pleasure of eating solid food.

During your fast, you may have your struggles, discomforts, spiritual victories, and failures. In the morning you may feel like you are on top of the world, but by evening you may be wrestling with the flesh-sorely tempted to raid the refrigerator and counting how many more days are left in your fast. This is especially true if you are new at fasting. To counteract temptations like these, take extra time with the Lord to spend with God. Step outside for fresh air and a moderate walk of a mile or two, and talk to the Lord as you walk along. And in the process always keep on sipping water or juice frequently during your waking hours.

All the experts agree that "breaking the fast" is the critical phase of fasting. While your body is in the resting mode, your stomach shrinks and your intestines become idle, so solid food must be re-introduced very slowly to avoid kidney failure or digestive distress. In fact, after a 40-day fast, you should make a careful transition for at least three days before return in to eating meats or fats or normal foods.

Further, if you end your fast gradually, the beneficial physical and spiritual effects will linger for days. But if you rush into solid foods, you may lose much of your deep sense of peace and experience physical problems such as diarrhea, sickness, fainting, and frankly even death in some cases, due to shock!

Dr. Paul Bragg and his daughter Patricia have conducted fasting clinics for many years. Their book, The Miracle of Fasting, gives a specific daily food plan for breaking a 7-day fast that could be adapted and stretched out over several more days for a 40-day fast.

Breaking a Seven-Day Fast

5 o'clock as you end your 7th day of the fast
- Peal four or five medium-sized tomatoes - cut them up, bring them to a boil and then turn off the heat. When they are cool enough to eat, have as many as you desire.

Morning of the 8th day

- Salad of grated carrots and grated cabbage, with half an orange squeezed over it.
- Bowl of steamed greens and peeled tomatoes (spinach, Swiss chard, or mustard greens). Bring the greens to a boil, and then turn off the heat.
- You may eat two slices of 100 percent whole-wheat bread, which has been toasted until it is thoroughly dry-this is called "Melba toast." After it has been cooled, the toast should be so dry that it would powder if you squeezed it in the palm of your hand. As I have stated, this first food should be in the morning.
- During the day, you may have all the distilled water you wish to drink.
- For dinner, you may have a salad of grated carrots, chopped celery and cabbage, with orange juice for dressing. This will be followed by two cooked vegetables, one such as spinach, kale, shard, or mustard greens, and one such as string beans, carrots, steamed celery, okra, or squash. You may have two pieces of whole-grain "Melba toast." These meals are not to contain oils of any kind.

Morning of the 9th day

- You may have a dish of any kind of fresh fruit, such as banana, pineapple, orange, sliced grapefruit, or sliced apples. You may sprinkle this with two tablespoonfuls of raw wheat germ, and sweeten it with honey, but not over one tablespoonful
- At noon you may have a salad of grated carrots, cabbage, and celery, with one cooked vegetable and one slice of "Melba toast."
- At dinner you may have a salad dish of lettuce, watercress, parsley, and tomatoes, and two cooked vegetables.

Most experts agree that breaking a fast with vegetables, either steamed or raw, is best. Your stomach is smaller now, so eat lightly. Stop before you feel full. Stay away from starches like pastas, potatoes, rice, or bread (except for "Melba toast") for at least a week. Also avoid meats, dairy products, and any fats or oils for a week or more. Introduce them very slowly and in small amounts.

Extended fasts are not the only fasts which need to be ended with caution. Even a 3-day fast requires reasonable precautions. It is wise to start with a little soup -- something thin and nourishing such as vegetable broth made from onion, celery, potatoes, and carrots -- and fresh fruits such as watermelon and cantaloupe.

In terms of resuming any sort of exercise routine, the advice is the same. Start out slowly, allowing time for your body to re-adjust to its usual regime.

APPENDIX III

Prayer Life

"Prayer is the natural outgushing of a soul in communion with Jesus."

– Spurgeon (Editor, Robert Hall), *The Power of Prayer in a Believer's Life*, p.30

Prayer and Fasting: Tool for a Successful New Journey

Prayer Life of Jesus "The Model Prayer"

Most Christians refer to Matthew 6:9-15 as "The Lord's Prayer." However, it is found in John, 17 where Jesus prayed in the Garden of Gethsemane. He was preparing to go to Calvary to die for the sins of the world. So, what was the purpose of Jesus' prayer in Matthew 6:9-15? It was to teach us how to pray, thus it "The Model Prayer."

As we travel on *The New Journey* employing "The Model Prayer", God's power will be given to us from on high like we have never witnessed in our lives. We will be able to achieve success at the next level in our journey with God, not because we are perfect people, but because we now know how to pray with power and purpose. That is why James the Elder declares in agreement with Christ, the Son of God; "*Prayer is powerful and effective.*" [12] Listen now to the teaching Christ provides in "The Model Prayer."

Read and Meditate on Matthew 6:6-15

"But when you pray, go into your private room, shut your door, and pray to your Father who is in secret. And your Father who sees in secret will reward you. When you pray, don't babble like the idolaters, since they imagine they'll be heard for their many words. Don't be like them, because your

---

[12]James 5:16b, says, "The effectual fervent prayer of a righteous man availeth much." The word "availeth" suggests to the travelers that this type of prayer gets the job done.

Father knows the things you need before you ask Him. Therefore, you should pray like this: Our Father in heaven, Your name be honored as holy. Your kingdom come. Your will be done on earth as it is in heaven. Give us today our daily bread. And forgive us our debts, as we also have forgiven our debtors. And do not bring us into temptation, but deliver us from the evil one. For Yours is the kingdom and the power and the glory forever. Amen. For if you forgive people their wrongdoing, your heavenly Father will forgive you as well. But if you don't forgive people, your Father will not forgive your wrongdoing."

WHEN WE PRAY

This is how the Lord Jesus Christ instructed His disciples to pray while on the journey. He did not tell them this was the only way to pray. Rather, He told them this was an effective way to pray:

"Our Father in heaven..."

This has to do with our God. It reveals His exalted position. He sits in Heaven watching over us. He cares and understands us. He is always there for us in times of need throughout *The New Journey.*

"...Hallowed be your name..."

This has to do with the holiness of God. God is holy and His name is holy. When we pray we are to respect and reverence His wonderful, mighty and glorious name. To disrespect His name cripples us on our *New Journey.*

"…Your kingdom come…"

This demonstrates God's dynamic dominion. God is at work building His Kingdom in each of us. As we pray, we begin to long for the coming of God's Kingdom. *The New Journey* is long and often difficult, but our eyes are fixed on the Kingdom, we know His Kingdom will come. Wherever the Kingdom of God is, peace and rest is found. Richard J. Foster in his magnificent work, *Prayer: Finding The Heart's True Home,* writes the following concerning the prayer of rest.

> Through the Prayer of Rest God places his children in the eye of the storm. When all around us is chaos and confusion, deep within we know stability and serenity. In the midst of intense personal struggle we are still and relaxed. While a thousand frustrations seek to distract us, we remain focused and attentive. This is the fruit of the Prayer of Rest.[13]

When we pray for the coming of His Kingdom, we are praying for all God is to us as His chosen people. The blessing is ours. God's kingdom will come. Remain focused.

"…Your will be done on earth as it is in heaven."

The New Journey is all about doing God's will. The will of God is an expression of the heart of God's deepest desire for His people and denotes two key concepts of His eternal nature: the "Perfect Will of God" and the "Permissive Will of God." The Perfect Will of God is what God dearly wants for all of His creation. God wants us to rest and be at peace in His Perfect Will. The Permissive Will of God, on the other hand, is an expression of man's free will. God gives us free will to embrace or not to embrace His Perfect Will. God gives us a choice

[13]Richard J. Foster, *Prayer: Finding The Heart's True Home* (New York: HarperCollins Publishers, 1992), p.93.

and does not force us to do what He wants us to do. He simply provides the opportunity for us to make choices. In Genesis 3, Adam and Eve did not choose God's best. They chose sin and their willful act of disobedience led to their expulsion from the Garden of Eden. How do we avoid our own "Edenmistic"[14] expulsion? We must learn to submit our will daily to the will of God.

"Give us this day our daily bread."

Our daily bread is our food for *The New Journey.* Like the manna of God, we have the living bread of eternal life in Jesus Christ our Lord. Eating this bread comes through daily feeding on God's Holy Word.

During our time of fasting and prayer, we need the Word of God to feed us until we want no more. We want Jesus to fill us with more of God and less of us so we might know Him more and serve Him better.

"Forgive us our debts, as we also have forgiven our debtors."

A debt is an infraction or a sin against either God or Man. Sin strains our relationship with God and our *New Journey* becomes more difficult. As Christians, we do not lose our salvation, but we do lose the closeness of our fellowship with Almighty God thus our *New Journey* becomes more stressful. Holding debts is not good for our Christian witness or our spiritual and physical health. This is why Jesus admonishes us to forgive one another. As we learn to forgive each other of the wrong done to us, we are saying to God, "Dear Lord, as I have forgiven others, please forgive me."

---

[14]"Edenmistic" is a word expression denoting the character of Adam and Eve following the fall in Genesis 3. Genesis 3:1, says, "Now the serpent…" (NIV). Sin entered the Garden of Eden, and man fell into sinful disobedience and God expelled mankind from paradise. Romans 5:12 says, "Therefore, just as sin entered the world through one man, and death through sin, and in this way death came to all men, because all sinned" (NIV).

As we focus on staying on *The New Journey,* let us learn the power of forgiveness and do for others what our Lord and Savior Jesus Christ did for us at Calvary. Christ died physically because He was fully human and He died to self because He put His Heavenly Father's will before His own. Therefore, we must also die to self. Death to self promotes success on *The New Journey.*

"And lead us not into temptation, but deliver us from the evil one."

Deliverance from self into the Savior is what we need. *The New Journey* makes deliverance a reality. Temptations, trials and testing come, but serious *New Journey* travelers know deliverance from bondage is at our fingertips. Persistent travelers remain confident that God is our Deliverer and His deliverance will always be on time. When His deliverance arrives, His power crushes the presence and power of the evil one (Satan, Lucifer, and the Devil), who is the Prince of Darkness and Deception (Ephesians 6).

"For if you forgive men when they sin against you, your heavenly Father will also forgive you."

To have a successful *New Journey,* employ the personal choice of forgiveness because it works and complete peace results. We all need peace – with ourselves, with others and with God. Finding peace is like uncovering precious jewels. Our *New Journey* is all of God and none of Man. Man is a sinner in need of forgiveness. Once forgiven by God, Man is responsible for doing for others what Jesus did – forgive! When we exercise the power of forgiveness, our *New Journey* will become a joy and not a job. Do not wait to be forgiven. Forgive even when forgiveness has not been received.

*"But if you do not forgive men their sins,
your Father will not forgive your sins."*

If we do not forgive, do not expect God to restore fellowship with us. When we refuse to be a forgiver, our *New Journey* will be hard and the road to success will not be paved with peace. Forgiveness allows God to do a new thing in and through us each day. *The New Journey* is where we can find power, peace and the Person of Jesus Christ. There is no other way to wholeness and holiness than being connected with God!

THE WONDERFUL NATURE OF THE NEW JOURNEY

What a wonderful place to begin *The New Journey* with God! Prepare to come into the presence of our Heavenly Father. He is waiting with great anticipation. Develop the discipline of spending quality time with the Lord in prayer as a lifestyle. Spend time in prayer with your immediate family as well. Educate them as to why fasting and prayer are so important to a follower of the Lord Jesus Christ. Allow questions and do not worry if answers are not immediately known. Take them to God in prayer.

This is a wonderful new spiritual journey to wholeness and holiness. God wants us to know beyond any doubt that we can be made "whole" (John 5). In fact, *The New Journey* is a whole life made complete in God. To continue this wonderful, new spiritual journey we must:

Awaken!

Ask God to awaken our soul and ready our heart to meet with Him face to face. Always keep prayer the focal point of your *New Journey.* Pray for at least seven people each week while traveling with God. Contact them by phone, text, email, Facebook or other social media. Offer them words of encouragement. Remember, when we seek God on our knees, the unity of the Spirit is kept through the bonds of peace (Eph. 4).

Know the Enemy!

Ask God to bind the Enemy from distracting us from our special time with our Heavenly Father.

Anticipate the Rewards!

Go to bed anticipating the rewards of time together with our Lord God.

Thank God Now!

Thank God in advance for what He is going to do in our life and in the lives of those we pray for.

Engage in Daily Acts of Kindness!

Consider seven acts of kindness to share every week. Daily kindness will bless all involved.

Trust God Wholeheartedly!

Ask God to enable us to trust Him with all our heart while giving us opportunities to share our faith with others.

Celebrate an Awakened Soul!

Praise God daily for awakening our soul! Enjoy God's anticipation of spending time with us and praise His name!

Be a Traveler!

Jesus Christ is God's "only begotten Son.[15]" the Second Person of the "Godhead."[16] We need to remember Jesus is always present as we daily seek God's heart. Look for God's activity while we journey and do what Christ commands, "Seek and ye shall find, knock and the door shall be open."[17] There is an expression which comes to mind from my childhood, "Trust in the Lord with all your heart, my son, and never depend on human knowledge, intellectual understanding or earthly insight, but only on God in three Persons: Father, Son and Holy Spirit."[18] Such trust elevates one's joy, peace, patience, love[19] and humility by causing the human soul to be at rest completely in God's sovereign presence and awesome power.

Be Personal with God!

It is my pastoral prayer that the Lord Jesus Christ will help every one of us to understand it is possible to travel *The New Journey* successfully when God is our source strength. God will not let us down. He is always there to help us in the Person of the Holy Spirit. God gave us His Son and He sent us God's Spirit to make sure we have a successful journey.

Be Made Whole!

This is why Jesus said to the lame man at the pool of Bethesda, "Do you want to be made whole?" (John 5:6b, NIV). As we travel, God's Holy Spirit challenges us to the wholeness we need. May God bless us and keep us in His eternal care. May His Love give us all we need to successfully complete our journey. Remember, Love is the most excellent way! Jesus is also asking us, "Do you want to be made whole"? If we do, let's respond with "Yes, Lord, make me whole!" He will answer our prayer.

---

[15] John 3:16, "Jesus Christ, God's Son."

[16] The Godhead is a term denoting God in three persons: God the Father, God the Son and God the Holy Spirit. See, Matthew 3:13-17. "Jesus" is the Son. "A voice from heaven" is the Father. And finally, "the Spirit of God descending like a dove" is the Holy Spirit.

[17] Matthew 7:7, "Seek God," (paraphrased).   [18] This is a saying from my childhood.

[19] Galatians 5:22-23, "The Fruit of the Spirit," refers to ones character. God develops human character, as we remain faithful in continuing to travel on the journey to wholeness and holiness.

APPENDIX IV

Be
Holy

Holiness Leads to Wholeness

Wholeness and holiness are what we passionately desire as we travel on this path as *New Journey* travelers. Jesus Christ, the Great Physician and Master Healer, is asking us like the lame man at the Pool of Bethesda the same penetrating question, "Wilt thou be made whole?"[22] Our "yes" may be the first step in our spiritual journey either individually or as a congregation. Plunging into the spiritual depth of the loving arms of the Lord of the Sabbath and witnessing the power and presence of God will change our life and our church. We will experience God's glory in a new and fresh way.

I sincerely pray the Lord Jesus Christ shows us individually and as a church how He wants us to travel on the path to wholeness and holiness. I pray the power and movement of the Holy Spirit helps us appreciate and enjoy a closer walk with Him. I am humbly praying we are able to shout praises with great joy.

Hear Our Prayer O Lord! Make Us Whole

Dear Lord, we are your people and want to be made whole.
Lead us and make us new.
Fill us with Your Spirit.
Heal us. Prepare us to meet You each day on Your terms.
Dear Lord, there is no one like You.
So, yes, Lord! We want to be made completely whole.
Amen and Praise God!

What is Our Focus?

Our focus on this adventure is to grasp the heart and soul of how Jesus makes the lame whole. As God's people, we need wholeness and holiness. When stepping out in faith in the Lord of the Sabbath as

---

[22]John 5:6, KJV.

journey travelers, the joy in John 5:1–16 will burst forth from our inner being. *The New Journey* is a journey to be fully enjoyed. We are indeed the people of God and we are entering into wholeness and holiness right now. Our objective is simple: "*Take up your bed and walk*" (John 5:8). Are you ready to begin?

Change Me O Lord! Change Me, I pray!

This devotional book seeks to enhance your time with God each morning and throughout the entire day. Pray earnestly and see how God changes your heart and habits.

Changing Habits and Starting Disciplines

You will be changing habits and some may be lifelong habits. Like any new discipline, this will take effort. Do not be discouraged if you do not experience immediate gratification. Continue to be faithful to the journey and the rewards will come.

Finding a Quiet Place

Go to bed early for the best early morning times with God. Find a quiet place for your meeting with Him.

Winning the War of the Flesh

Understand Satan and the flesh will war against our spirit in the days ahead. Satan will try to distract us and at times we may think things are actually getting worse. Remember God is on our side. We are more than conquerors (Romans 8:37).

Remaining Committed to God's Word

Let others help us. Stay in regular contact with those who are in contact with God. Stay in His Word every day. Do not miss times of inspiration, encouragement, worship, fellowship and discipleship in small groups. God wants to nurture and love us with Tender Loving Care (TLC). This is agapé love (i.e., the love of God, John 3:16-17). Keep a spiritual journal and be determined to cross the finish line. Pay the price. Let the Lord lead and keep the faith. We can make it. God is on our side because we are in Christ (2 Corinthians 5:17). We will begin to notice a difference in our lives. God will change us, our habits and our hearts, and give us the mind of Christ. Wholeness in Christ will emerge. The inner being of our soul will become the outer dress of our Spirit-anointed radiance.

Enjoying Freedom in His Presence

This devotional book is simply a guide for our journey. Let the Lord lead us into His wonderful and magnificent presence. Do not let this devotional book bind us. Allow the Holy Spirit to remain in charge throughout the entire journey. God knows what He is doing. Remember He is God! He is the ultimate Guide. Our goal is to glorify Him and develop intimacy with the Person of the Lord Jesus Christ.

Being Holy!

The Bible teaches us to be holy instead of engaging in unholy things or activities. Holiness is more than activity; it is a matter of the wholeness of our heart. When our hearts are wholly bent toward God's Heavenly throne, we are holy. The Apostle Paul correctly encouraged and admonished us to be holy.

Holiness does not imply being absolutely perfect. Holiness suggests being set apart for service unto both God and Man. Holiness is God's way of separating us from the ways of the world. We are in the world, yet we are not of the world. We are the righteousness of God, made anew daily by God's amazing grace and loving-kindness. We belong to God and were purchased by the blood of Jesus at the cross on Golgotha's hill. Whole and holy, that's who we are. Let us exalt Him as the Lord of the Sabbath today and every day.

Practicing God Exalted Living!

"Wherefore God also hath highly exalted him, and given him a name which is above every name: That at the name of Jesus every knee should bow, of things in heaven, and things in earth, and things under the earth; And that every tongue should confess that Jesus Christ is Lord, to the glory of God the Father" (Philippians 2:9-11).

Exalt Christ and be holy! Proceed for the glory of God!

APPENDIX V

Scriptures
and
Strongholds

Scriptures for Fasting and Breaking Spiritual Strongholds

When sensing a biblical need to fast and break a spiritual stronghold, meditate on the following Scriptures. The Holy Spirit of God will prepare your heart for victory.

1. **Nehemiah 9:1** *"Now in the twenty and fourth day of this month the children of Israel were assembled with fasting, and with sackclothes, and earth upon them."* Confronted with insurmountable challenges, Nehemiah called the children of Israel to a solemn assembly to fast and pray. What do you do when you are faced with insurmountable challenges in your life?

2. **Esther 4:3** *"And in every province, whithersoever the king's commandment and his decree came, there was great mourning among the Jews, and fasting, and weeping, and wailing; and many lay in sackcloth and ashes."* Fasting, weeping and wailing in sackcloth and ashes, were the Jews best defense. What is your best defense during heart wrenching times?

3. **Esther 9:31** *"To confirm these days of Purim in their times appointed, according as Mordecai the Jew and Esther the queen had enjoined them, and as they had decreed for themselves and for their seed, the matters of the fastings and their cry."* Mordecai and Esther understood the significance of fasting and crying out to the LORD God Almighty. Do you understand the significance of fasting and crying out to the LORD God Almighty for help in times of despair and disillusionment?

4. **Psalm 35:13** *"But as for me, when they were sick, my clothing was sackcloth: I humbled my soul with fasting; and my prayer returned into mine own bosom."* We must choose to seek God. Seeking God is an act of humility. Fasting was an illustration of the Psalmist's seeking the wisdom of God. Do you seek God in all things or does it require profuse pain in your soul before you acknowledge your need of Him?

5. **Psalm 69:10** *"When I wept, and chastened my soul with fasting, that was to my reproach."*

6. **Psalm 109:24** *"My knees are weak through fasting; and my flesh faileth of fatness."*

7. **Jeremiah 36:6** *"Therefore go thou, and read in the roll, which thou hast written from my mouth, the words of the LORD in the ears of the people in the LORD's house upon the fasting day: and also thou shalt read them in the ears of all Judah that come out of their cities."*

8. **Daniel 6:18** *"Then the king went to his palace, and passed the night fasting: neither were instruments of musick brought before him: and his sleep went from him."*

9. **Daniel 9:3** *"And I set my face unto the Lord God, to seek by prayer and supplications, with fasting, and sackcloth, and ashes..."*

10. **Joel 2:12** *"Therefore also now, saith the LORD, turn ye even to me with all your heart, and with fasting, and with weeping, and with mourning..."*

11. **Matthew 15:32** *"Then Jesus called his disciples unto him, and said, I have compassion on the multitude, because they continue with me now three days, and have nothing to eat: and I will not send them away fasting, lest they faint in the way."*

12. **Matthew 17:21** *"Howbeit this kind goeth not out but by prayer and fasting."*

13. **Mark 8:3** *"And if I send them away fasting to their own houses, they will faint by the way: for divers of them came from far."*

14. **Mark 9:29** *"And he said unto them, This kind can come forth by nothing, but by prayer and fasting."*

15. **Luke 2:37** *"And she was a widow of about fourscore and four years, which departed not from the temple, but served God with fastings and prayers night and day."*

16. **Acts 10:30** *"And Cornelius said, Four days ago I was fasting until this hour; and at the ninth hour I prayed in my house, and, behold, a man stood before me in bright clothing,"*

17. **Acts 14:23** *"And when they had ordained them elders in every church, and had prayed with fasting, they commended them to the Lord, on whom they believed."*

18. **Acts 27:33** *"And while the day was coming on, Paul besought them all to take meat, saying, This day is the fourteenth day that ye have tarried and continued fasting, having taken nothing."*

19. **1 Corinthians 7:5** *"Defraud ye not one the other, except it be with consent for a time, that ye may give yourselves to fasting and prayer; and come together again, that Satan tempt you not for your incontinency."*

20. **2 Corinthians 6:5** *"In stripes, in imprisonments, in tumults, in labours, in watchings, in fastings;"*

21. **2 Corinthians 11:27** *"In weariness and painfulness, in watchings often, in hunger and thirst, in fastings often, in cold and nakedness."*

Fasting Approach: Food Guidelines

I discovered these food guidelines while completing a doctoral level seminar on Spiritual Disciplines. Following the seminar, I began to apply the disciplines of fasting, praying and food selection during my personal time of devotion to the Lord. The food guidelines proved so successful that I decided to incorporate these guidelines in each of my books on fasting and praying. The objective in refraining from eating certain kinds of meat proved challenging and exciting. The food guidelines are to be used throughout the entire forty day period of fasting and prayer.

1. No beef.
2. No pork.
3. No lamb.
4. The fast allows for eating fish and fowls.
5. The fast allows for eating wheat and other natural grain/bread products.
6. No fried fish or fowl, vegetables or bread products.
7. No candy or desserts. Gum and breath mints are permitted.
8. The fast allows for eating fruit (fresh/canned in natural juices or lite/frozen and the like).
9. The fast allows for drinking all types of juices (Kool-Aid® without sugar).
10. Cold tea, hot tea and coffee are permitted without processed sugar (Equal® and related are permitted).

Note: As with any significant dietary change, please consult your physician or healthcare professional, especially if you have diabetes, are pregnant or nursing.

Breaking Spiritual Strongholds

1. **Psalm 35:13** *"But as for me, when they were sick, my clothing was sackcloth: I humbled my soul with fasting; and my prayer returned into mine own bosom."*

2. **Daniel 9:3** *"And I set my face unto the Lord God, to seek by prayer and supplications, with fasting, and sackcloth, and ashes…"*

3. **Matthew 17:21** *"Howbeit this kind goeth not out but by prayer and fasting."*

4. **Mark 9:29** *"And he said unto them, This kind can come forth by nothing, but by prayer and fasting."*

5. **Luke 2:37** *"And she was a widow of about fourscore and four years, which departed not from the temple, but served God with fastings and prayers night and day."*

6. **1 Corinthians 7:5** *"Defraud ye not one the other, except it be with consent for a time, that ye may give yourselves to fasting and prayer; and come together again, that Satan tempt you not for your incontinency."*

APPENDIX VI

Tools
for the
Journey

13 Tools for Dealing with Anger
(A Self Examination)

1. **Proverbs 14:29** *"He that is slow to wrath is of great understanding: but he that is hasty of spirit exalteth folly."*

   Examination Question: Do you consider yourself an angry person who has a habit of venting and projecting your anger onto others before you know it?

2. **Proverbs 15:1** *"A soft answer turneth away wrath: but grievous words stir up anger."*

   Examination Question: How do you feel when you actually turn away from wrath?

3. **Proverbs 22:24-25** *"Make no friendship with an angry man; and with a furious man thou shalt not go Lest thou learn his ways, and get a snare to thy soul."*

   Examination Question: Do you seek to develop friendships with angry people?

4. **Ecclesiastes 7:9** *"Be not hasty in thy spirit to be angry: for anger resteth in the bosom of fools."*

   Examination Question: What happens when you act before before you think?

5. **Matthew 5:22** *"But I say unto you, That whosoever is angry with his brother without a cause shall be in danger of the judgment: and whosoever shall say to his brother, Raca, shall be in danger of the council: but whosoever shall say Thou fool, shall be in danger of hell fire."*

   Examination Question: What does it mean to be angry with your brother or sister without a cause?

6. **Galatians 5:19-21** *"Now the works of the flesh are manifest, which are these; Adultery, fornication, uncleanness, lasciviousness, Idolatry, witchcraft, hatred, variance, emulations, wrath, strife, seditions, heresies, Envyings, murders, drunkenness, revellings, and such like: of the which I ell you before as I have also told you in time past that they which do such things shall not inherit the kingdom of God."*

   Examination Question: If you have ever seen these qualities in a Christian or fellow church member before, how did it make you feel about that person?

7. **Ephesians 4:26** *"Be ye angry and sin not: let not the sun go down upon your wrath:..."*

   Examination Question: How is it possible to be angry and sin not?

8. **Ephesians 4:31** *"Let all bitterness, and wrath, and anger, and clamour, and evil speaking, be put away from you, with all malice:..."*

   Examination Question: How do you successfully put away these ungodly qualities?

9. **Ephesians 6:4** *"And, ye fathers, provoke not your children to wrath: but bring them up in the nurture and admonition of the Lord.*

   Examination Question: Do you, as a parent, have a habit of provoking your children?

10. **Colossians 3:8** *"But now ye also put off all these; anger, wrath, malice, blasphemy, filthy communication out of your mouth."*

    Examination Question: What does a person need to do to rid themselves of these ungodly qualities?

11. **1 Timothy 2:8** *"I will therefore that men pray every where, lifting up holy hands, without wrath and doubting."*

    Examination Question: Why do you think Paul shared this desire with his protégé, Timothy?

12. **Titus 1:7** *"For a bishop must be blameless, as the steward of God; not selfwilled, not soon angry, not given to wine, no striker, not given to filthy lucre;..."*

    Examination Question: Do you understand the importance of these qualities described in Paul's letter to Titus?

13. **James 1:19-20** *"Wherefore, my beloved brethren, let every man be swift to hear, slow to speak, slow to wrath: For the wrath of man worketh not the righteousness of God."*

    Examination Question: Do you consider yourself a person who knows how to weigh your words before speaking them?

Seven Tools for Dealing with Anxiety

(A Self Examination)

1. **Proverbs 3:24** "*When thou liest down thou shalt not be afraid yea, thou shalt lie down and thy sleep shall be sweet.*"

    Examination Question: Are you an anxious person?

2. **Matthew 6:25-34** "*Therefore I say unto you, Take no thought for your life, what ye shall eat, or what ye shall drink; nor yet for your body, what ye shall put on. Is not the life more than meat, and the body than raiment? Behold the fowls of the air: for they sow not, neither do they reap nor gather into barns; yet your heavenly Father feedeth them. Are ye not much better than they? Which of you by taking thought can add one cubit unto his stature? And why take ye thought for raiment? Consider the lilies of the field, how they grow; they toil not, neither do they spin: And yet I say unto you, That even Solomon in all his glory was not arrayed like one of these. Wherefore, if God so clothe the grass of the field, which to day is, and tomorrow is cast into the oven, shall he not much more clothe you, O ye of little faith? Therefore take no thought saying What shall we eat? or, What shall we drink? or, Wherewithal shall we be clothed? (For after all these things do the Gentiles seek:) for your heavenly Father knoweth that ye have need of all these things. But seek ye first the kingdom of God, and his righteousness; and all these things shall be added unto you. Take therefore no thought for the morrow: for the morrow shall take thought for the things of itself. Sufficient unto the day is the evil thereof.*"

    Examination Question: As you look at yourself ,do you find yourself anxious about the next day?

249

3. **John 14:1** *"Let not your heart be troubled: ye believe in God, believe also in me."*

   Examination Question: Do you show signs of having a troubled heart?

4. **John 14:27** *"Peace I leave with you, my peace I give unto you: not as the world giveth, give I unto you. Let not your heart be troubled, neither let it be afraid."*

   Examination Question: Are you a person of peace or do you see possess a troubled heart and/or mind?"

5. **Philippians 4:6** *"Be careful for nothing; but in every thing by prayer and supplication with thanksgiving let your requests be made known unto God. And the peace of God, which passeth all understanding, shall keep your hearts and minds through Christ Jesus."*

   Examination Question: How does this Scripture passage speak of you?

6. **Colossians 3:15** *"And let the peace of God rule in your hearts, to the which also ye are called in one body; and be ye thankful."*

   Examination Question: Is your spirit one with the Spirit of the Lord or do you have a divided spirit?

7. **1 Peter 5:7** *"Casting all your care upon him; for he careth for you."*

   Examination Question: Do you feel in your heart the Lord truly cares for you?

Six Tools for Dealing with Unforgiveness

(A Self Examination)

1. **Matthew 6:12** *"And forgive us our debts, as we forgive our debtors."*

   Examination Question: Do you find it difficult to forgive others who have offended you?

2. **Matthew 7:1-5** *"Judge not, that ye be not judged. For with what judgment ye judge, ye shall be judged: and with what measure ye mete, it shall be measured to you again. And why beholdest thou the mote that is in thy brother's eye, but considerest not the beam that is in thine own eye? Or how wilt thou say to thy brother, Let me pull out the mote out of thine eye; and, behold a beam is in thine own eye? Thou hypocrite, first cast out the beam out of thine own eye; and then shalt thou see clearly to cast out the mote out of thy brother's eye."*

   Examination Question: Are you judgmental?

3. **Matthew 18:32-35** *"Then his lord, after that he had called him, said unto him, O thou wicked servant, I forgave thee all that debt, because thou desiredst me: Shouldest not thou also have had compassion on thy fellow servant, even as I had pity on thee? And his lord was wroth, and delivered him to the tormentors, till he should pay all that was due unto him. So likewise shall my heavenly Father do also unto you, if ye from your hearts forgive not every one his brother their trespasses."*

   Examination Question: Why do we find it so difficult to forgive others while wanting immediate forgiveness from Christ for ourselves?

4. **Ephesians 4:29-32** *"Let no corrupt communication proceed out of your mouth, but that which is good to the use of edifying, that it may minister grace unto the hearers. And grieve not the holy Spirit of God, whereby ye are sealed unto the day of redemption. Let all bitterness, and wrath, and anger, and clamour, and evil speaking, be put away from you, with all malice: And be ye kind one to another, tenderhearted, forgiving one another, even as God for Christ's sake hath forgiven you."*

    Examination Question: Have you ever had corrupt communication proceed out of your mouth?

5. **Colossians 3:12-13 (NASB)** *"So, as those who have been chosen of God, holy and beloved, put on a heart of compassion, kindness, humility, gentleness and patience; bearing with one another, and forgiving each other, whoever has a complaint against anyone; just as the Lord forgave you, so also should you."*

    Examination Question: At what level do you possess these holy and beloved qualities God put in your heart: compassion, kindness, humility, gentleness, patience and bearing with one another in forgiveness?

6. **James 5:9** *"Grudge not one against another, brethren, lest ye be condemned: behold, the judge standeth before the door."*

    Examination Question: Should a Christian to hold a grudge?

Nine Tools for Dealing with the Tongue

(A Self Examination)

1. **Proverbs 10:19** *"In the multitude of words there wanteth not sin: but he that refraineth his lips is wise."*

   Examination Question: Do you consider yourself a person who knows how to wisely control your tongue?

2. **Proverbs 12:18** *"There is that speaketh like the piercings of a sword but the tongue of the wise is health."*

   Examination Question: Do you believe your tongue is a healthy tongue?

3. **Proverbs 17:28** *"Even a fool, when he holdeth his peace, is counted wise: and he that shutteth his lips is esteemed a man of understanding."*

   Examination Question: Have you ever experienced a time in your life as a Christian where you lost control of your tongue?

4. **Proverbs 21:23** *"Whoso keepeth his mouth and his tongue keepeth his soul from troubles."*

   Examination Question: What personal things does this Proverb say to you?

5. **Ephesians 4:29-30** *"Let no corrupt communication proceed out of your mouth, but that which is good to the use of edifying, that it may minister grace unto the hearers. And grieve not the holy Spirit of God, whereby ye are sealed unto the day of redemption."*

   Examination Question: Have you been living according to this passage or have you grieved the Holy Spirit?

6. **James 1:19-21** *"Wherefore, my beloved brethren, let every man be swift to hear, slow to speak, slow to wrath: For the wrath of man worketh not the righteousness of God. Wherefore lay apart all filthiness and superfluity of naughtiness, and receive with meekness the engrafted word, which is able to save your souls."*

   Examination Question: Are you slow to speak and quick to listen?

7. **James 1:26-27** *"If any man among you seem to be religious, and bridleth not his tongue, but deceiveth his own heart, this man's religion is vain. Pure religion and undefiled before God and the Father is this, To visit the fatherless and widows in their affliction, and to keep himself unspotted from the world."*

   Examination Question: According to this passage of Scripture, are you a religious person?

8. **James 3:2-8** *"For in many things we offend all. If any man offend not in word, the same is a perfect man, and able also to bridle the whole body. Behold we put bits in the horses' mouths, that they may obey us; and we turn about their whole body. Behold also the ships, which though they be so great, and are driven of fierce winds, yet are they turned about with a very small helm, whithersoever the governor listeth. Even so the tongue is a little member, and boasteth great things. Behold how great a matter a little fire kindleth! And the tongue is a fire, a world of iniquity: so is the tongue among our members, that it defileth the whole body, and setteth on fire the course of nature; and it is set on fire of hell. For every kind of beasts, and of birds, and of serpents, and of things in the sea, is tamed, and hath been tamed of mankind: But the tongue can no man tame; it is an unruly evil, full of deadly poison."*

   Examination Question: Why do you think it is so difficult to control the tongue?

9. **James 3:9-14** *"Therewith bless we God, even the Father; and therewith curse we men, which are made after the similitude of God. Out of the same mouth proceedeth blessing and cursing. My brethren, these things ought not so to be. Doth a fountain send forth at the same place sweet water and bitter? Can the fig tree, my brethren, bear olive berries? either a vine, figs? so can no fountain both yield salt water and fresh. Who is a wise man and endued with knowledge among you? let him shew out of a good conversation his works with meekness of wisdom. But if ye have bitter envying and strife in your hearts, glory not, and lie not against the truth."*

Examination Question: How is it possible, yet problematic, that from the same mouth proceeds both blessing and cursing?

APPENDIX VII

Continuing the Journey (CTJ)

The New Journey has only just begun!

Read the CTJ Scripture passages. Pause to meditate on and memorize each passage. Express ways you plan to continue your *New Journey to Wholeness and Holiness.*

"If my people, which are called by my name, shall humble themselves, and pray, and seek my face, and turn from their wicked ways; then will I hear from heaven, and will forgive their sin, and will heal their land."

(2 Chronicles 7:14)

"But seek ye first the kingdom of God, and his righteousness; and all these things shall be added unto you. Take therefore no thought for the morrow: for the morrow shall take thought for the things of itself."

(Matthew 6:33-34a)

"Ask, and it shall be given you; seek, and ye shall find; knock, and it shall be opened unto you: For every one that asketh receiveth; and he that seeketh findeth; and to him that knocketh it shall be opened."

(Matthew 7:7-8)

"If ye abide in me, and my words abide in you, ye shall ask what ye will, and it shall be done unto you. Herein is my Father glorified, that ye bear much fruit; so shall ye be my disciples."

(John 15:7-8)

"Trust in the LORD with all thine heart; and lean not unto thine own understanding. In all thy ways acknowledge him, and he shall direct thy paths. Be not wise in thine own eyes: fear the LORD, and depart from evil."

(Proverbs 3:5-7)

--------------------------------- • **CTJ** • ---------------------------------

"And he shall be like a tree planted by the rivers of water, that bringeth forth his fruit in his season; his leaf also shall not wither; and whatsoever he doeth shall prosper."

(Psalm 1:3)

--------------------------------- • **CTJ** • ---------------------------------

"Therefore the ungodly shall not stand in the judgment, nor sinners in the congregation of the righteous."

(Psalm 1:5)

--------------------------------- • **CTJ** • ---------------------------------

"For the LORD knoweth the way of the righteous: but the way of the un godly shall perish."

(Psalm 1:6)

Prayer Disciples Prayer List

_____

_____

_____

_____

_____

_____

_____

_____

_____

_____

_____

_____

_____

_____

_____

_____

_____

_____

_____

_____

_____

Prayer Disciples Prayer List

About the Author

Robert F. Loggins, Sr. was born in Winona, Mississippi, but considers Laurel, MS his hometown. His educational background includes:
- Bachelor of Science degree from University of Southern Mississippi
- Master of Divinity from New Orleans Theological Seminary
- Doctor of Ministry program at Midwestern Theological Seminary (MBTS). Currently enrolled and was MBT Oxford University Scholar in 2010

Bob has served the Lord Jesus Christ in various roles including:
- Pastor of churches in Mississippi, Louisiana and Missouri
- Church Planter
- Missionary
- Greek, Baptist History and Philosophy instructor at Union Theological Seminary in partnership with NOBTS
- Prayer and Spiritual Awakening Specialist for the Missouri Baptist Convention and North American Mission Board
- Member of Missouri National Day of Prayer
- Board member of Fellowship of Christian Athletes
- Chapel preacher for the St. Louis Rams and St. Louis Cardinals
- Camp pastor for Ponca Bible Camp

Bob currently serves as:
- President and Founder of R. F. Loggins, Sr., Ministries, LLC, an outreach, teaching, equipping and coaching ministry
- Executive Director of Mission Metro St. Louis, a transformational ministry to over 4,000 churches promoting Christian unity, prayer and cooperative leadership
- Author of Christian growth books including:
  - *The New Journey to Wholeness and Holiness*
  - *The Journey to Wholeness and Holiness*
  - *Preaching for Spiritual Awakening*
  - *The Good News Soul Winning Daily Devotional Manual*

Bob and his wife, Cassandra, have been married for 35 years and have two sons, Robert Jr. (wife, Maria) and Jordan. They are also the proud grandparents of Madison Taylor (7 yrs.), Christopher Ellis (5 yrs.) and Garrison Frank (4 mo.).

Join the Journey Team

Schedule a Journey Workshop House of Prayer (JWHP)
- One Day Workshop
- Weekend Prayer & Spiritual Awakening Church Leadership Retreat
- One Hour of Power

Consider Scheduling these Conference and Prayer Event Options:
- Spiritual Awakening and Revival Meetings
- Associational Prayer and Spiritual Awakening Vision Casting
- College and University Walls of Jericho Prayer Walking Rally
- An Inner Life Discipleship Prayer and Devotional Retreat
- Youth and Teens 40 Day Prayer and Fasting Commitment Period–Feeling Peer Pressure? Apply Prayer Pressure!
- Church and Associational Prayer Altars, Prayer Rooms and Prayer Teaching
- The Road Block Series to Revival and Spiritual Awakening
- When Husbands and Wives Bow: Spiritual Renewal Through Prayer
- When Families Pray Together
- How to Pray Your Way Through Change
- Transforming Business Meetings Into Blessing Meetings Through Prayer and Fasting
- When Children Learn How to Pray With Purpose: How to Pray For Bullies and over Boohoos
- Wholeness and Holiness: Identifying and Breaking Spiritual Bondage
- How to Pray for Rain: The Prayer Foundation of a Church's Building Program and Financial Stewardship
- How to Become a One Spirit Church Through Prayer
- How to Pray All Night

For More Information

For additional copies of *The New Journey to Wholeness & Holiness* or scheduling events, contact Pastor Bob Loggins at:

ROBERT F. LOGGINS, SR., MINISTRIES, LLC

15917 Eagle Chase Court
Chesterfield, Missouri 63017

robertlogginsp@yahoo.com

www.PastorLoggins.org

Obey the Great Commission to GO – Matthew 28:18–20

Practice the Greatest Commandment to LOVE – Matthew 22:37–40

Remember the Great Confession to PRAY – 2 Chronicles 7:14

GO, LOVE and PRAY for REVIVAL and SPIRITUAL AWAKENING

PrayerDiscipleship™ Notes

PrayerDiscipleship™ Notes

PrayerDiscipleship™ Notes

PrayerDiscipleship™ Notes

PrayerDiscipleship™ Notes

_____

_____

_____

_____

_____

_____

_____

_____

_____

_____

_____

_____

_____

_____

_____

_____

_____

_____

_____

_____

_____

_____

PrayerDiscipleship™ Notes

PrayerDiscipleship™ Notes

PrayerDiscipleship™ Notes

PrayerDiscipleship™ Notes

PrayerDiscipleship™ Notes

PrayerDiscipleship™ Notes

PrayerDiscipleship™ Notes

_____

_____

_____

_____

_____

_____

_____

_____

_____

_____

_____

_____

_____

_____

_____

_____

_____

_____

_____

_____

_____

_____

_____

PrayerDiscipleship™ Notes

PrayerDiscipleship™ Notes